Jubilee

Enjoy 50 Stories From 50 Years Of Life

written by

LuAnn Joyce Caperton

Edited by

Barbara Horner Joyce

WestBow
P R E S S
A DIVISION OF THOMAS NELSON

C.S. Lewis Quotes, Thomas Payne, Reverend B.R. Hicks, Max Lucado, Joyce Meyer, Rick Warren, Father's Love Letter used by permission Father Heart Communications ©1999-2011 FathersLoveLetter.com

www.Jubilee50years.com

WestBow Press books may be ordered through booksellers or by contacting:

WestBow Press
A Division of Thomas Nelson
1663 Liberty Drive
Bloomington, IN 47403
www.westbowpress.com
1-(866) 928-1240

ISBN: 978-1-4497-3468-8 (hc)
ISBN: 978-1-4497-3467-1 (sc)
ISBN: 978-1-4497-3466-4 (e)
Library of Congress Control Number: 2011962757

Printed in the United States of America

WestBow Press rev. date: 01/16/2012

Table Of Contents

Highest Praise and Thanks goes to:

The LORD Jesus Christ

Who makes all things possible

Thanks also goes to:

Carlos Caperton
for his encouragement & support

Dad & Mom
who taught me about Jesus & His Love

Kathy, Joshua & Krista
for allowing me to share their stories

Samanda & Samantha
for giving me the love of two more children

Cathy Mays
for being everything an awesome sister could be

David Joyce
for being a brother that encourages chasing every dream

Aunt Polly
for using your gift of "strength" for eternal purposes

Aunt Jean
for using your gift of "creativity" to give me self-confidence

Sharon Crowley
for saying 100 times "You need to write a book" among other things

Linda Rumple
for looking at me through the eyes of Jesus

B.R.Hicks
For sacrificing so much to bring us the Bride's Message

The many Pastors & Teachers
Who gave of their time to teach me & others
about our LORD & Savior, JESUS CHRIST

Miracles are a retelling in small letters of

the very same story

which is written across the whole world

in letters too large for some of us to see.

C.S.Lewis

Preface

I know I am not the only one who has had a life full of "Ups & Downs". Surely, you can "Relate". But, as you will read in the following pages, when things began to go from bad to worse, in my "average, everyday life", I began to wonder why. "Was I doing something to cause this turmoil, or was I just looking at life's curveballs in the wrong way?"

While seeking an answer to this question, well, I guess you could say, "The Answer sought me." I began to realize, that I was placing all my energy into "getting what I wanted", whether it be "Possessions, Acceptance or Love"; they all were the things I desired. They were what actually "Ruled Me". Mostly, if I have to admit it, out of the three I just named, Love was the one I sought most; And I tried to find it in many places.

Why am I telling you all this? There's only one reason why. I want you to find the Answer; or for the Answer to find you. My hope, my desire, is that you, throughout these pages, whether you are 8 or 80, find what you have been searching for all your life.

I share this collection of fifty stories with you today, so that perhaps you will find yourself, your situation, among the many pages, and that they will take you, like me, from Toddler, through Tragedy, and to Triumph.

Introduction

Please join us as we walk through the life experiences of just one of the many individuals, who desire to express their gratitude to the Lord and Savior, Jesus Christ.

Finding grace and mercy; forgiveness and healing, LuAnn uses her own shortcomings, downfalls, and realizations, to show you the many examples of how this God of the Universe, relates, sees and cares for even the smallest of us.

At age 50, LuAnn has chosen, to share this Jubilee, in celebration and thanks for God's Gift of His Son, Jesus Christ, and the Redemption He brings to each of us.

In this stack of letter filled pages, there are a mere 50 out the large collection of wondrous stories of how the LORD has ministered to her, while walking through everyday life.

Many, O LORD my God, are thy wonderful works
which thou hast done,
And thy thoughts which are to us-ward:
They cannot be reckoned up in order unto thee:
If I would declare and speak of them, they are more
than can be numbered.
Psalm 40:5

LuAnn's hopes are, that somewhere in these simple, yet heartfelt words to follow, that your hope in Christ will either be found for the first time, or strengthened in some way, by what you read.

Chapter One

When & If

I will praise thee; for I am fearfully and wonderfully made: marvelous are thy works; and that my soul knoweth right well. Psalms 139:14

Let's begin this story, in the beginning, shall we? It was 1959. Thomas and Barbara Joyce had been married for 4 years, and as many couples do, they began to believe that life was about something more than waking, working, eating and sleeping. The longing for creating and nurturing another life, made between them, began to grow. Thomas and Barbara agreed to start a family.

Barbara & Thomas Joyce

After 12 consecutive months of anticipation then disappointment, anticipation, then disappointment, Barbara began to wonder if she would ever hold in her arms, a little one of her own.

As a couple, they chose to seek medical advice to see if there was anything they could do to improve their chances of conceiving, then went back to the drawing board to try again.

Desperately, one day, Barbara prayed . . . . "Lord, if you will just grant me this one request, a child of my own, I promise, I will give that child back to you." And not long after Barbara had prayed . . . the LORD amazingly gave Barbara her first child. On January 3, 1961, a baby girl was born. They named her LuAnn. That was me.

Although I was Thomas and Barbara's first child, I would not be the first grandchild for their parents to celebrate, but both sets of Grandmas and Grandpas were happy just the same. They encouraged and 'loved on' this new little family, which soon grew from just the three of them, to four then five. Thomas and Barbara were blessed with two more children, Cathy and David.

Thomas and Barbara had their hands full then. While Thomas worked hard at Western Electric as a "Tester", Barbara stayed home to be "Tested", by their little ones!

In the summer of 1966, the Joyces decided to take a vacation from those everyday "Testings". Their children were ages 5, 3, and 2 years old.

The Smiths, some longtime friends of the Joyces, lived in New Jersey and had extended an invitation up to visit. The Joyces had planned their time away from home well. They saved money and planned the trip in detail. The week finally arrived to load the 'anything and everything' one might need for a family of 5 to travel and vacation for 7 days. A relative had even added a big box of strawberries to deliver to the Smiths. Dad was especially glad to be able to drive the 9 hour trip in his "New To Them" Chevrolet BelAir purchased only two weeks prior. It was a shiny Meadow Green Metallic color and just a smooth ride with floor mats to match!

Knowing that it was more than a 300 mile drive to the Smith's home in N.J., Thomas wanted to get to bed early and rise early to take that long drive; But friends had come to visit the night prior to leaving. Thomas got in bed around 9:30 pm but only tossed and turned sleeplessly. Adjusting his family's original plans, to leave in the morning, he woke them from their sleep during the night. Everyone piled into the "New To Them" automobile. Thomas, my Dad drove first, as he and Mom had agreed to share the responsibility. Dad switched places with his wife after a while. It wasn't long before she became weary and her eyes unmistakably heavy. She handed the driving duties back over to her husband. It would be only hours later that we hit the guardrail on an interstate in Pennsylvania. The whole family had fallen asleep. It was somewhere around sunrise when the once beauty of a BelAir had become just a heap of torn scrap metal. My Mother recalls waking to the horrifying sound of metal twisting in front of and under her. Her legs, cramped between the front seat and the dash, were quickly unfolded as Dad took my brother from her arms. Little David, who had been in her lap, had no visible injury. Cathy, my sister had been in the backseat. She sustained a bloody lip, and Dad and I walked away unscathed. Mama took her little ones into the high grass in a nearby field, to empty their now nervous and full bladders, while the appropriate emergency vehicles arrived. Other than the car being estimated a "total loss", and the large box of strawberries having to be left behind, my family had been brought through this accident thankful; still breathing and clinging to one another.

The Highway Patrol Personnel gave us a ride to the nearest town and dropped us off at a Diner for some breakfast. I was only 5, but can most certainly recall it being my first time using the mini cereal box, turned on its side and torn opened, as a bowl to add milk to. As a kid who hadn't seen too much in her short life, I was amazed!

After a small breakfast on shaky stomachs, Ronnie Smith picked the Joyce family up in his station wagon, and took them safely the remaining 120 miles to his family's home.

From top to bottom step:
Pam Smith, Lee Smith, LuAnn, Cathy and David Joyce

Trying to make the best of the rocky-started vacation, our parents continued on as planned and took us to a zoo. I remember seeing my very first peacock there. It's deep, shiny array of colors made it extra beautiful to me. Mom shared with me, as she retells the story, that somewhere along the way that day, we must have eaten some bad food, because all of us became very sick.

After only a few days with the ailing, yet hospitable Smith Family, Thomas and Barbara decided to take in a couple of quick sites in New York with their children, and then catch a bus from there and return home. While at the bus station, we loaded onto the 'Greyhound' and into our 4 reserved seats. David sat on Mama's lap and his sisters with their "Daddy" nearby.

An auto accident, then getting ill from bad food; Whew! "What *else* could possibly happen?" you might be asking, at this point in the story. Well, you just *had* to ask ....Yep; we weren't home yet.

During the bus ride home, there was a "Switch" of buses required for this trip. And at the station where the "change over" was to take place, there were more folks wanting to get on, than the number of seats available. Dad had both Cathy and I clutched by his sides as he desperately attempted to get onboard. Once he was on, he turned and realized that the bus was filling up fast. As the bus driver called out, "I have one more seat left" to the crowd below that were bunched up in an unorganized shuffle. Dad yelled out, "Please, just get my wife on this bus!" Mom and little David were allowed to fill that last seat. It was a long ride home. Mom says her chest hurt for days afterwards from David's head resting on her while he slept.

We were picked up in Greensboro at the bus station, by my uncle J.B. (my Dad's brother) and were finally back home. Every one of us got over our sickness, and eventually recuperated from the long, exhausting trip. Outwardly, there was little difference in this Joyce family, but inwardly, some things had been changed.

Chapter Two

He Still Speaks

For I know the thoughts that I think toward you, saith the LORD, thoughts of peace, and not of evil, to give you an expected end. Jeremiah 29:11

After returning home from our New Jersey trip, my Dad purchased another Chevrolet; it was a Nova, of the same color as the BelAir! Things were getting pretty much back to a regular routine for the Joyce household, but my Mom, whose schedule was the busiest of all, had not been herself since our time in New Jersey. She later described it as this *gnawing or tugging* inside. She wasn't scared or upset or having "flashbacks" . . . none of that, just a bothersome question in her gut. Something in her life was missing. She shares, "I should have been the happiest woman alive! I had a husband that loved me, who worked very hard to provide for us, 3 loving little children and a home to call our own. I couldn't figure out why I wasn't happy." she said.

I had been in first grade for 2 months. And even with the one less child underfoot for 6 hours a day, still, she could not understand what it was that would not let her soul rest.

My Aunt Polly (Dad's sister) had been attending church for a while. She had been a real "piece of work" in her days. Being a Tomboy in earlier years, a strong will had followed her into her teens and twenties. She was feisty and funny, and one that spoke her mind always. But since she had started going to church, and had been talking about this person JESUS, there had been some kind of radical change . . . Polly was living a life for God now; she was even asking people to come to a revival that her church was having. Two of the people she asked to come were my Dad and Mom!

As they sat on a pew in this large and beautiful church called "Andrews", they found themselves so captivated by what the Evangelist was preaching, that they decided to return another night. Dad was really busy most evenings because he worked on the side as an umpire for the local softball and basketball teams, so Mom knew that this was an unusual circumstance. They heard a lot of Word in those 2 nights at revival, but after that, they went about their own lives and routines as usual. Mom continued to feel unsettled and far from content.

**Pictured above: Grandma Joyce, Aunt Jean,
Barbara (my Mom), Aunt Glenda and Aunt Polly**

My Aunt Polly had a strong will . . . . Did I mention that already? She was still going to that church of hers and had been praying for her brother and his wife; "Tom and Bobbie", as she affectionately called them. So when they announced at "Andrews" that "High Attendance Sunday" was drawing near, Polly jumped like a "soldier with a mission to complete", and once again asked Dad and Mom to come and "help her fill a pew"!

They accepted the invitation and visited "Andrews" once again, but when leaving Sunday School to go into the Sanctuary that morning, they found that there were no seats left on the lower floor, so up to the balcony they went.

The choir and congregation sang wonderful songs celebrating the Lord's mercy and grace, and the message shared by Don Carter from God's Word touched my Mama's heart. She had felt all this time that she was a *good* person; why, they had even attended a local church pretty regular, but there had definitely been something missing.

So nearing the end of the service that day, Mama knew at the moment the "alter call" began, that she needed to go to the front and talk to someone about that "missing something".

The first verse of the hymn, "Just As I Am", was nearly over and Mom was trying to get up from her seat in the balcony, but she knew there was a set of steep stairs that she would need to descend to get to the lower level. Mom tells how the enemy whispered in her ear each time she began to stand, "If you try to go to that alter, you're going to fall down those stairs . . . you're going to make a fool of yourself . . ." On and on he continued, putting fear and doubts in her mind. Desperately, Mom stood and told him under her breath, "I don't care if I *do* fall! I MUST get to that alter!"

The LORD must have rolled out the red carpet for my mama that day, for she made her way down with no incident at all . . . and when she got there, someone told her all about how JESUS loves her and how He paid the price for her sins already, and that all she had to do was accept His gift to her. She left with her family that day, knowing that she had JESUS in her heart. The void she had felt for so long was now filled with Jesus' Glorious Life, Light and Love!

My Mom was amazed at the way her life was changing. Many days and weeks had passed since she had asked JESUS into her heart. She may not have known it at the time, but she had become the Spiritual leader of our family. Now, she wanted to learn more of His Word, and be around others that loved the LORD. Our family began attending Andrews Memorial Baptist Church each week.

After Christmas, and all our celebration of Jesus' Birth, we had become pretty comfortable at "Andrews". Mom had been praying for Dad and I'm sure Polly had also. My Daddy was *and is* a strong, independent man, with a great mind and lots of athletic abilities. It's those kind of people, the one's who are self-sufficient and that seemingly "have it all worked out", especially those that believe "I am a good person", like my Mom, that find no need of a Savior. But one Sunday, Preacher Eugene Hancock had been speaking from the pulpit and during his sermon, actually came down to where the congregation was sitting, and walked straight to my Dad and asked, "Son, don't you want to give your heart to JESUS and serve the LORD with your wife?". Dad stepped out from his pew and followed the assistant pastor Don Carter through a door that led to the back. Some of the ladies of the church came to mom after service and expressed their excitement about Dad going to talk with someone about Salvation. They noticed, however, that Mom wasn't sharing the joy, as they had expected. When the ladies asked, "Aren't you happy that your husband went with him? Her response was, "I just don't know." (Thinking to herself, "He may have felt forced or persuaded"), "We'll see when he comes out", she added.

Mom had so much hope inside that Dad was truly going to give his life to the LORD, but she knew how strong and independent he was. By asking JESUS to come into his heart, it would mean admitting that he was "in need". But all doubts were washed away from my Mom's thoughts, when Dad came back out into the sanctuary to meet her. He quickly walked up to where she stood and hugged her saying, "Thanks so much for praying for me." Mom was blessed that day, to know that she not only had a wonderful husband, but a husband whose heart and soul belonged to God.

After they returned home, Dad phoned his sister, Polly. Although Polly had been out of town and had missed church at Andrews that day, he knew she would be at their Dad and Mom's house having lunch, as she did most Sundays. Polly answered her parent's phone and found Dad on the other end. "Hello?" Dad began to speak as he was wearing a wide grin: "Hi sis! I just wanted to let you know, that today in church, they found a sinner sitting in the 7th row". Polly was so ecstatic! She was shouting and rejoicing along with all those angels the Bible talks about when one sinner gets saved!

It was a precious, precious time in Dad and Mom's lives. Now, together, they could walk with the LORD.

Chapter Three

Lead, & They Will Follow

But Jesus said, Suffer little children, and forbid them not, to come unto me: for of such is the kingdom of heaven. Matthew 19:14

Days, weeks and months went by as Dad and Mom lived, learned and grew in their faith. But being a Christian doesn't mean life's going to always be "peaches and cream". Some people talk about the friends that were suddenly unavailable for cookouts or even family members that gave them a hard time about their faith, but Dad and Mom ? They say that most of their family and friends were Christians even before *they* made that Eternal choice, so they had a lot of encouragement and support after they gave their lives to Christ.

Dad and Mom tell of times they were able to share their faith with some of their unsaved friends. Overall, they seemed very interested in what was being shared. My parents laugh, as they tell of the time they were at some friend's for a cookout and a swim; Mom was having such deep discussions of the gospel with one of them, that she forgot about the meal! Dad and the other person got tired of waiting for them to finish their in-depth talk, so they just started eating without them!

Getting back to tough instances though; I do remember the times they used to talk about; the way the Devil would fight them every Sunday morning as they attempted to get themselves and us kids ready to go to church. It was probably like one of those bad dreams where you need to run, but your body will only move in slow motion.

They tell that once we arrived at the church though, all would be well; but the onslaught of deterring hindrances prior to getting out of the driveway was horrendous.

"It was all worth the effort", Mom says. They learned so much from Don Carter and Betty Futrell, some of their Sunday school teachers and of course Pastor Hancock.

Left to right: Cathy, LuAnn, and David

My brother, sister and I had our own little classes to attend. One of my favorite teachers was in my earliest years there. Her name was Mrs. Crouse. I looked forward to seeing her each week. There couldn't have been more than 6 or 8 of us in her small, colorful classroom upstairs. As we sat at a little round table, she would have us join hands and pray. And whether we colored a pretty picture, sang songs or listened to one of her adventurous stories from God's Word, we would always go away with more than we arrived with. She continually planted the seeds of Christ's love that I hungered for then, and the ones I would surely need for later.

Sometimes, after Sunday school with Mrs. Crouse, we would have literature to take home with us. I remember, in particular, one night, my Mom picked up one of the "Send home papers". On the front it had the word "STANDARD" and a picture of a parent and child.

Mom, who was my faithful bedtime story reader, picked up the thin paper from my bedside and began to read it to me. Tucked into my warm covers, I listened to her words intently. The story was about a child that had learned from his mother how much Jesus loved him. The boy, in the story's end, had asked Jesus into his heart. As Mama's voice dropped and faded, assuming I would be quite sleepy by this time, I surprised her. I had one question on my mind.

"Mama, can I ask Jesus into *my* heart too?" My mother, with a sweet and assuring voice, led her 6 year old daughter through the sinner's prayer.

I don't know how I went to sleep that night; for I was so excited. In the morning, as I woke, I became happy all over again! I had asked Jesus into my heart!

It was Wednesday, and that night our family attended services at church. After the adult class was over, my mother came to get me from the children's building where I had been learning about God on my own level. As we walked hand in hand along the "drive" that led to the main parking lot, the Pastor came out of another door, and walked alongside us. "Preacher Hancock! Preacher Hancock! Guess what happened last night!" I exclaimed. "Well, I don't know, little one, why don't you tell me?" He replied with a smile, looking up at my Mom, seeing hers.

"I asked JESUS into my heart, Preacher Hancock! I got saved!" I announced with joy.

Preacher Hancock, still grinning, congratulated me, and added more encouraging words. But I didn't realize how touched he was with the "6 year old's" enthusiasm and testimony until he shared it with the congregation on Sunday. He preached about "Coming as a child" to Jesus, and challenged each person to have "that kind of jubilance for their own salvation". Of course, I was totally unaware of all he had said during the service about that little girl that had approached him on Wednesday night. I was probably busy coloring or just trying my best to stay quiet while the adults learned. Mom shared the story with me after church that day.

My sister and brother came to know JESUS not long after that, through Dad and Mom's faithfulness to get us to church and their prayers.

Chapter Four

Trains, Bikes & Monkeys

. . . Whosoever shall receive this child in my name receiveth me: and whosoever shall receive me receiveth him that sent me: for he that is least among you all, the same shall be great. Luke 9:48

You must remember that I *was* young at one time. And as much as we would like to believe that children don't really know or understand much about the world that awaits them out there as they get older, they do pick up on things; they do know and understand more than we give them credit for. It's sad, in a way, for as parents, our hopes are to shield them from harm and hurt, problems and pain. But we cannot be everywhere for everyone at all times, let's face it: Only God is omnipresent.

That's why it is so important to "train up a child in the way he should go" as *Proverbs 22:6* commands us to do. *Train up a child in the way he should go: and when he is old, he will not depart from it.*

Their surroundings, their education, your parenting, means everything to their futures. Remember, you don't have to be a teacher to teach, you don't have to be a Mother, to mother, you need not be a Father to father. Look at your children, look at the children around you, and know, that they are the leaders of tomorrow.

I have no explanation for what may have prompted the following dream, but the vividness and purity of it has survived quite a long time and remained nestled inside my heart and head for over 40 years. Please allow me to share:

I must have been around 7, when in my sleep; I met a boy my age. He was sitting at the front part of a train, like an engineer. His train

14

stopped in front of me as I stood gazing at him. He talked with me, but I cannot recall the majority of the conversation. I just remember the awesomeness of Love I felt from Him.

He loved me just the way I was. He looked at me through passionate eyes. He saw everything I was and wasn't . . . and still, He loved me. When His train started up again, as to continue on its path . . . on the tracks laid before it, I was distraught at His leaving. I ran after him, begging desperately that He not leave me. With the same compassion He'd shared through His eyes, He spoke and assured me that He would be back for me.

I still cry each time I recall the dream; I am crying now.

The LORD taught me early on, to trust Him. Oh, the dilemmas of childhood:

I had been riding my bicycle for quite a while with training wheels on, and it was time to "graduate" to bigger and better things. My Dad took off the training wheels for me and "viola"; I was able to peddle on my way, wobbly but without incident. I was doing well on level road or sidewalk, but when the challenge of staying on my bike, while going down our hilly driveway . . . . uh—uh. No way. I was too afraid to even attempt it. The driveway, to an adult, may have looked like a "breeze" to tackle, but to an inexperienced 7 year old? Huh . . . all 45 degrees of incline might as well have been the incline of a roller coaster at an amusement park! I wasn't about to take THAT on; not yet.

During my sleep one night, just as vividly as the dream prior to this one, I saw myself get on that little red bicycle, start at the top of that huge "mound of a hill" driveway, and take off riding down it. The moment I woke that morning, I threw my "outdoor" clothes on, flung open the door leading out to the carport, walked my bike up the hill, turned it, facing that GREAT CHALLENGE, and WOW !!! I rode it all the way down! Jumping off my bike, I ran into the house shouting! I did it! I did it! I rode down the hill without falling! It was in my dream!

The LORD loves His children. And what is important to a little one, is important to Him.

I'm sure you remember some of the teachers you have had in school. Maybe it was the way they talked, the way they wore their hair, or their wardrobe that you remember.

Ms. Hunter, my 3rd grade teacher, however, was a thin black woman, and best remembered for her great big beaming smile. She was firm, yet positive in the way she spoke to the students in our class. I respected her greatly; Well, I guess, as much as an 9 year old can respect someone.

We had gone through much of the school year, learning basic Reading, Writing and Arithmetic. I had been a quiet, shy type of student during my long 3 year stint at Grove Park Elementary School. (except for an incident with combing my hair for Picture Day, before Ms. Waynick had given us permission to do so.)

But today, we were learning about a subject my teacher called Evolution. Ms. Hunter went on to explain what Froude said about "from where" and "how" we "came to be". I sat curiously listening to our lesson.

After school let out that day, and when I had arrived home, I began asking my Mom how it was that we came from "monkeys" and such.

I had just received a new Bible of my own. It was red leather bound with my name on the right lower portion of the cover. My Mom opened my Bible with me and showed me where I could find the Truth about how I was made, and from where I came.

I must have taken God's Word very serious for my age, because although I had only been a Christian for 2 years, I can see now how the LORD had built my faith and trust in Him and His Word quickly.

Underlining the appropriate verses, I placed my Bible into my satchel. I was determined, that on the next school day, I was going to share with my kind, yet misinformed 3rd grade teacher, this Truth from God's Word.

My words were that of a 9 year old, and I do remember telling her that my Father was not a monkey, but for however the conversation went that day, I have not forgotten how Ms. Hunter still shared her Big Beaming Smile on her kind, dark face, with me, as she showed attentiveness and grace while I pointed out to her, *Genesis 1:26-27.*

*And God said, Let us make man in our image, after our likeness:
and let them have dominion over the fish of the sea, and over the
fowl of the air, and over the cattle, and over all the earth, and over
every creeping thing that creepeth upon the earth.
So God created man in his own image, in the image of God created
he him; male and female created he them.*

As a child I loved the Lord, for as much as I knew Him. I looked forward to practicing his ways, and sharing His Love with others. He provided lots of opportunities to learn and implement those things I had learned.

Four or Five of our neighbors were Christians. They demonstrated many times for me how Christian's lives *should* and *could be* like: Barbara and Bill Durham, two of those neighbors, held Bible Studies and Special Prayer Meetings in their home. I attended some of them with my mother. There, I learned how to pray, and saw examples of how the Holy Spirit moves people to tears!

Amena, the lady who lived behind us, held a week of Vacation Bible School at her home one summer. She needed to have invitations to that VBS, distributed to all the young children like me in the surrounding neighborhood. With permission from my mom, I told her I would deliver them. Each day since she had asked for my help, it had rained. It rained hard. But being just as "strong willed" as my Dad and Aunt Polly, I knew I had a job to do, so I took my 'little girl umbrella', and walked from house to house to house, until all the invitations had been delivered. I had no idea that my determination would earn, from Amena, a reward! On the last day of our VBS, she presented me with an old emptied cigar box, and in it was the largest bag of M&Ms I had ever seen! "My! Isn't God good?" I must have been thinking.

Then, there was Pastor Styles. He and his family lived right beside us! They were kind folks; always smiling and busy helping people. When I saw them mowing their yard a few times, I ran inside and brought out to them a glass of cold iced water. I suppose I had been learning about the scripture:

> *For whosoever shall give you a cup of water to drink in my name,*
> *because ye belong to Christ, verily I say unto you, he shall not lose*
> *his reward. Mark 9:41*

I wasn't anyone special in that of myself, but I knew I was special to God. And that, my friend, to the small and great, to the rich and poor, and to the young and old, is inspiration enough to believe one can move mountains.

Has this world been so kind to you that you

should leave with regret?

There are better things ahead than any we

leave behind.

C.S. Lewis

Chapter Five

Trusting No One &
Not To Be Trusted

For out of the heart proceed evil thoughts, murders, adulteries, fornications, thefts, false witness, blasphemies: These are the things which defile a man. Matthew 15:19-20a

Fast forwarding through the years of ups and downs including becoming an Elementary Safety Guard, then dealing with Middle School Bus Bullies, and the whole awkward year at age 13, let's make a stop in 1975, shall we?

As my class was completing our 8th grade year, the School System of Burlington decided they would combine all upcoming 9th graders to one central location. That location was Sellars Gunn.

Dad and Mom did not like the location of the school; But me? At age 14, who's thinking about 'location'? I found at my new school, there were new people to meet, a selection of classes and hobbies, and even choices on your lunch tray! Oh, and plenty of boys to get to know! Huh. Wow. I sound like I really was a socialite. Nope. I mostly stayed by myself except the occasional pajama party at a girlfriend's house.

At first, going to this controversial school was pretty cool, but it was none too soon, that I found myself surrounded by kids my age that were "hard to read" and "downright unpredictable". Take my friend Jimmy, for instance. He was just a "Cool Cat", trying to make the best of the year like the rest of us. Probably just as shy as I was to begin with, but to "fit in" he decided to use other students as human sacrifices. No . . . . not that he killed them, but, well, almost.

There was a tall, thin and confident looking girl, with sandy blonde hair named Kathleen. Jimmy hung out with her. *I only knew her by* acquaintance. One day, Kathleen was talking with Jimmy. Jimmy had told her that someone had made the statement that she acted like a B★%#^ ! When Kathleen put the "heavy hand" on him to tell her who it was, he said, "It was LuAnn!" I don't know if someone had actually called her that name or not, but now that Jimmy had opened that door, he was going to need a scapegoat quickly! And the "scapegoat" he picked was *me*!

The next day, Jimmy hesitantly informed me that Kathleen might be looking for me, and that I should be aware that she thinks I called her a B★%#@. "Why does she believe THAT??!" I exclaimed. "Well, because I told her that." He explained. Man, I could not understand for the life of me why he would make up such craziness! You see, Kathleen wasn't your typical 14 year old. She must've had a tough life so far, because she was known to carry knives to school with her. I was petrified!

Each day I went to school knowing that I would have to dodge her during class changes, on the ball fields and in the gymnasium and at special rallies and announcements. I was afraid of her, yet too scared to report the incident, and hoping and praying it would all "go away". I continued to plead with Jimmy to "fix this problem he'd cultivated".

Lunchtimes were the most hair-raising for me and my nerves, because Kathleen and I had the same lunch period. I came into the cafeteria each day with eyes peeled wide open and reflexes armed and ready . . . . To run!!

Finally, one day, Jimmy told me that he had explained everything to her and that she was not mad at me anymore. I was still a little "rattled" when the day came that she saw me in a crowd and walked over to talk with me. We ended up as friends, actually. Why, she even wrote in my yearbook!

I shared that story to lead up to this: When Williams and Cummings High Schools were planning a dance at the YMCA to take place after one of their football games that year, they handed out a special invitation to the 9th graders, that would be going into 10th grade at their schools the next year. A group of my regular "Pajama Party" girls were planning to go, with their parents as escorts and asked if I could go to the dance and then "sleep over" that night afterwards. My parents told me that I could not go.

After being in the "Jimmy and Kathleen" life and death situation I had come through, all I wanted was to be with friends and dance. I actually had had a big complex about dancing. I didn't know how to dance until just about a month earlier. I took the time to practice my "Moves and Grooves" with my girlfriends, and I'd wanted to go "test them out" on a real dance floor, with Boys even!!! But would my parents allow me to go? Their answer was still "N-O".

Lots of things after that seemed to be in accordance with the Domino Act . . . oh, I mean, you know . . . the Domino Effect. Things just weren't "going my way", so I ran away from home and spent the night outside in the cold, with my blanket, wind up alarm clock, and luggage hidden behind some bushes at a nearby church.

I was only caught and "told on" as I crossed a neighbor's yard the next morning. I had been making my way across that yard to the bus stop that would have taken me to school. What? You didn't think I was going to skip school, did you? Nope. That came much later . . . 12th grade.

Okay, so after I went back home from running away, our church split up. My friends went to another church while I remained with my family at "Andrews". Not long after that, my parents wanted to send my siblings and me to Christian School. In the interview with the principle, he asked me if I wanted to go to his school. I answered, "Well, I have been looking forward to going to my parents' high school, and I have already been to some of the football games" there. (speaking of Walter M. Williams)

I had no idea that my answer during that special interview would count me "Out" when acceptance and denial letters came in the mail that summer. Dad and Mom were crushed when they found that their oldest had not been accepted into the school. I did not know that in their precise planning, they had counted on me to drive David and Cathy *to* that Christian school each day.

I dated a few boys in 9th and 10th grade and "fell in love" with a boy named Wayne. And although we attended Sellars Gunn together, we had to go to separate high schools when it came time. He and I both found jobs at McDonald's Hamburgers.

One of the teachers I'd had in 11th grade D.E. (Distributive Education) class, allowed me to be her "assistant" or "helper", I guess you'd call it, when I'd moved into the 12th grade. Mrs. Vickie Hodge was a very intelligent woman in my eyes. But even with all the knowledge she'd impressed me with, it was her sense of "fairness" that struck a special chord in my heart. She was firm in her dealings with students, but had a discernment about her that gave her ability to tell when someone needed a little extra nudge or bit of advice to "get them through" a situation. She was neither extra harsh or overly gentle, but "Just right" . . . kind of like the bed that Goldilocks slept on. I felt more comfortable around her than any adult I had known so far in my life.

When I switched jobs twice trying to "have more time on the weekends for my boyfriend, Mrs. Hodge was "straight up" with me. She told me that I needed to be careful about my "job situation". It had something to do with "having a job" to receive a passing grade in her class. I appreciated her frankness without judgment. She didn't treat me like a child, but an adult. I could see that she wanted the best for me. She must have dealt with lots of teenagers in her many years as a teacher, for she seemed to understand the emotional rollercoaster we all were going through at that age.

During that senior year, Wayne told me that he wanted to date other people. I was sick inside. I'd gotten so used to being part of his family. We'd spoken many times of marriage after high school. I'd even imagined what our children were going to look like when they were young. What was I to do with my life now? (you know, all the things a "teen" feels when they are rejected) The break up was just another heavy brick added to my already suffering teenage emotional state of mind. I began to distrust people, and actually "hate". But the truth is that the person I really hated was me.

Weeks went by and I wasn't getting over this guy one bit; I felt like the walls at home were closing in on me, as I tried to forget how I'd felt about him. So, I went for a radical change; As soon as I turned 18, in January, I moved out of my family's home and in with my friend Crystal, and her Mom. I rented a room from them, (although I really was sharing the room with Crystal.) My new roommate kept me busy enough most of the time, and I wouldn't think of the things that were hurting me inside.

Crystal was a girl that "spoke her mind" always. When I first began living with her and her Mom, I didn't always *agree* with the way she acted. There were traits I simply didn't think I'd ever want to "take on" for myself. But the more I thought of how tough other people seemed to be, and the more I desired for the hurt of rejection to cease in me, the more desperate I became. I picked up a cigarette one day, and asked Crystal for a "light". That was the beginning of a long line of vices I'd have later.

But first, before I'd "give up on the world and what it had to offer"; I wanted to give this "marriage" thing a try. At age 18, just 2 months after graduation, I married a young man that I thought could heal all my hurts and settle this 'anger against the world' that I felt. Kevin was a nice man, 4 years my senior, and treated me well, but by this time, I had no self-respect. It felt like I didn't have an ounce of compassion left in me for the human race. I just could not seem to pull myself out of this pit of despair I'd fallen into. I was not satisfied; I was not happy.

While my good and faithful husband worked in Winston Salem 5 nights a week, I worked and hung out at Roll-about Skating Center. There, I met lots of folks that had the same "take" on life that I had recently developed. I became just *one of the crowd*. With drugs now available to me, I took "uppers" to make time fly by. I did so many things that I shouldn't have, to put it mildly. I didn't even have respect for the bonds of marriage. I left my husband when I was 20 with the excuse that I didn't love him like a wife ought to love her husband. I told him he deserved better. It was the "most honest" I had been with him since we'd come together.

After I totally gave in to all that anger inside me, I began to abuse my mind and body with drugs, "relations" with men, by drinking, smoking and using foul language. I cut my hair short and began to dress "tough"; With my cigarettes rolled up into the sleeve of my "muscle t-shirt" at times, I go with my friends to the local bar and "shoot pool". My favorite motto was "FTW". Yes, it was a sad, sad sight; that lost little girl named LuAnn Joyce.

But somewhere in the midst of all that darkness, that self-loathing misery, a small light of hope appeared one day. Yes, there were always people around me that would readily give me what I wanted; tell me what I wanted to hear, but there were also a couple that saw a teen in peril and used their God given abilities to steer me into a more constructive direction. Soon, after they got me on the right track, my trust issues began to change; I got arrested. "Wait!" you might be saying, "I thought you said, *"Soon after that my trust issues began to changed"*? Yes! Be patient! I'm getting there!

Chapter Six

A Glimmer Of Hope
Found In Justice

For there is nothing covered, that shall not be revealed; neither hid, that shall not be known.
Luke 12:2

I had been working a job in Physical Therapy as an Aide. It was quite the "step up" from my position at the Snack Bar at the Skating Rink. I had really been enjoying taking care of the injured and elderly patients there. As a pastime, I continued to use skating for exercise, for fun and to hang out with people I had met there during my employ. One such friend of mine was Bill.

Bill was a large and handsome man; he was as harmless as a kitten. Bill and I had a couple of things in common. We both were without a mate, and had some "lonely" time on our hands. We began to get closer and be more than just someone to fill each other's time. During the increased days I spent with him, however, I began to suffer some repercussions from his former wife.

Spring was nearing its end and the PT Dept. needed to cut some of their part timer's hours. The Director of Nurses at Skilled Nursing Division asked me if I would be interested in learning more about nursing, and fill in for some of the Aides who were needing vacation time during the summer months. I was glad to receive more training and be able to stay with the patients I already had grown fond of.

One warm summer evening, after those in our care had been assisted to their beds, some of the Nurse's Aides heard the honking of a car horn;

it was coming from the parking lot on the lower floor. As we gazed out the window from the level above, we observed a carload of young women yelling obscenities and flying finger gestures at us. It was Bill's "strange", I mean "estranged" wife. One of her friend's had called me at work earlier to tell me how distraught she was that I was dating Bill. I told her I was sorry and I thought she should to talk to him about it. I told her I couldn't stay on the phone while at work. She cussed me out and hung up.

A few days later, my sister called me from my parent's house and told me that a policeman had come by looking for me. Cathy told me that he'd said, "Please tell her it would be better if she comes to the Police Dept. herself, to take care of this matter." So, what did I do? I went.

The Officer that fingerprinted me was the same one that used to visit at the Skating Rink I worked at. Yes, you can close your mouth now, they *did* arrest me. He explained that I was to be "officially arrested", fingerprinted and charged with "Threatening another person's life". I was so confused. "Whose life did I threaten?" Yep. It was none other than the *"finger flicker"* in the Nursing Home parking lot. The police allowed me to leave the station that day with my signature on a document stating that I, agreed to show up for court on a specific day in July.

So, after many weeks had passed, of anxiety and dread, I came to the 'Courts' as required. In a large room, folks gathered to have attendance taken and then be split up into smaller courtrooms for hearings and such. The place was filling up quickly as the hour drew near for "roll call". Two blonde young women made their way through the crowd, and found empty seats on the row just in front of me. I recognized one of them as the "Finger Flicker"; the person that had brought these insane charges against me. She and her associate began to talk amongst themselves, as they looked around. "Do you see her?" "No, I don't see her yet." they exchanged. All the while, I was sitting directly behind them, hearing every word.

The official began to call the names. After several were announced, and hands were raised, I heard, "LuAnn Joyce?" "Here", I answered, as I lifted my hand in the air. They both turned slowly, with eyes widened and faces red. I just smiled.

Next, I was given a choice to have a court appointed attorney or hire my own. I chose a court appointed attorney. In a somewhat private area, they jotted down a few figures and told me that my income exceeded the limit on having one appointed. They politely informed me that if I was found guilty for this crime, the penalty was anywhere from a monetary fine to 2 years imprisonment. Then they asked if I wanted to postpone the hearing date to "find myself an attorney". I had been nervously awaiting the date of this confrontation and did not desire to put it off one more minute.

The officials led us to a smaller courtroom. Her attorney stood by her. I had brought a friend, so I had them and The Law on my side. I didn't deserve to ask the LORD to be on my side, so I didn't even attempt to pray. My life was still "Out Of Order", and I knew it, but this whole incident would bring me one step further down into the hole I was digging for myself.

The Judge listened to the charges and "FF's" attorney said some things, but when asked if I wanted to say anything in my defense, I took the stand alone. I was determined to set the record straight and let the Truth be made known.

I told the Judge and all present, if the Plaintiff was as afraid of me as she claimed to be, why had she come to my work, at a Healthcare facility, late at night, and honked, screamed and used obscene gestures for all the staff and patients to see? I was the one who had to be escorted to my car that night after work by security personnel after all. In closing, I asked the Judge, "If she is telling the truth about a threat made on her life, why won't she even look us in the eye? You must believe that she *is* lying." The Judge saw right through her act, dropped the charges on me and made her pay court costs and her attorney's fees. It was truly a day of celebration for me and my friend. Actually, this time of success brought us closer. This friends name was Dennis.

Dennis was someone I had known since I was 15. He had moved away and then moved back to this area again. We had lots of fun and went everywhere together. But just as quickly as he came back into my life, he was "out of it".

Dennis had worked for "Pic And Pay Shoes". He was offered a promotion to Store Manager, but would have to move to Roxboro to manage the store there. Dennis and I agreed to continue to date each other exclusively. He even took me to Roxboro to visit his new place several times. But one night, I tried to call him at our usual time to chat and he wasn't available. He called me later and told me he had been at the store until late. He didn't know that I had already called the store to ask if he was there. He came to see me that weekend and I asked him again where he had been that night I'd tried to call. He retold me the same story about a load of purses that had to be put on display. I then confronted him about my call to the store earlier. He hung his head in shame and admitted he had been seeing someone else. Once again, my point was proven: Why trust anyone? I added a couple of more vices to my list of cussing, drinking and smoking after that. Cigarettes had taken second place on my list of "smokes".

Chapter Seven

Mischief, Mayhem & Murder

I will bear the indignation of the LORD, because I have sinned against him, until he plead my cause, and execute judgment for me: he will bring me forth to the light, and I shall behold his righteousness. Micah 7:9

After continuing to fill my time with many more short romances and crazy parties, where I came away missing much sleep, jewelry, and other things, I began to "get tired of the madness".

I started enjoying the more simple things like working back in Physical Therapy, shining up my little red VW, paying my bills and hanging out with friends. I did simmer down a bit and spend my extra curricular time shooting billiards again at a place downtown. But then again, I was not totally free from poor decisions, for I found myself racing a friend's Jeep against a "supped up" truck off of Main Street, which was the popular drag.

While I was still living in my "angry little world", one of my friends happened to introduced me to his boss. This boss' name was Matt.

Matt seemed to be the responsible, down to earth type. He was a supervisor at his job and I admired him. Matt and I shared some of our "stories" while out together a few times. As we got to know each other, he told me that he had been separated from his wife for 10 months. After we had been seeing each other a while as more than friends, I discovered, just after my birthday in 1982, that I was pregnant. As Matt and I pondered and discussed the future of parenthood, I shunned at the thought of being pregnant and unmarried. I knew it would hurt my parents badly. Matt and I talked of getting married, but that's when I found out "The Lie". Matt hung his head; (much like Dennis had before), and confessed, that he had just separated from his wife when we met, so THAT meant, that by the time our baby was born, he would just be getting his divorce. I thought about going to live with my Godmother in another state until this little one inside me was born, but that thought was soon put to rest, by doubts that she may not take me in. So, to hide my sin, to prevent the shame, we chose to go to a clinic in Greensboro. After the first appointment, I was given a date shortly afterward to have this "procedure" done. On April 17, 1982, I laid on an examining table, while medical personnel dilated my cervix. The sound of a suction machine was turned on and the trained staff began to maneuver a long instrument in all directions. The hose to that instrument was connected to a machine while the other end was inside of me. In desperation for one last moment to halt this insane "choice" I had made, I screamed and cried, "No! No!; My baby! My baby!" They halted the machine, but only for a few moments so they could stop my thrashing. They told me it had to be finished; what had been started, and that I must remain still for the extent of it. As the machine was turned back on, I laid and cried, for I knew that they were extracting what remained of that little life I'd signed away, along with all its nourishment. I knew that this would be marked as the worst mistake I'd made in my 21 years.

With specific instructions on how to "take care of yourself" after the procedure, I was discharged. "*No Alcoholic Beverages for 48 hours*", the paper read. I had a friend take me straight to a Restaurant that served mixed drinks, and had one. I hated myself; who I had been and what I had become.

Chapter Eight

Mercy & Grace

And when these things begin to come to pass, then look up, and lift up your heads: for your redemption draweth nigh. Luke 21:28

After what I'd done to so far to ruin my life, this was by far the worst. I had thought I was only hurting myself as I lived the life of "freedom" they call it. But now, my eyes were open; I had taken the life of another; my own flesh and blood.

I was feeling the wretchedness of my sin and the hole my child had left inside of me. I was sick of me, I was sick of men and the pain the two joined together seemed to bring. I had wanted a child as far back as age 15, and here, when I was blessed with one, I had thrown it away.

Although Matt did not express much of his sadness, I knew it had changed his life in some ways. We stayed together, as he promised me a family, and in December of that same year, he and I were married. We had just a simple little ceremony in his sister's home with relatives and a couple of friends in attendance. His family was nice to me; down to earth folks with hardy laughs and great big hugs. Matt and I spent a lot of time with his Dad and Mom. We eventually moved to a house only a block over from theirs. I liked the feeling I got when I'd sit out on his parent's swing behind their house. They taught me how to relax, settle down, and enjoy the little things that life has to offer.

Somewhere in that time period, I worked at Dominos Pizza, and then I began to work as a cashier at Food Lion on Maple Avenue in Burlington. Matt was working there as a Stocker. We were a young and happy couple, just taking life one day at a time.

I began to think about other people more than about LuAnn, and had a desire to make a difference in people's lives, other than just ringing up and bagging groceries, so I talked with Matt about it, and he suggested I pursue a career in Cosmetology. Yes! I could use my training to change the way people feel about themselves! I had first hand experience with this, you see. Let me explain:

When I was about 14 years old, my family had taken a trip to the beach. While playing in the summer sun, my Mom sprayed some peroxide onto my hair. "Cool !" I thought as I looked in the mirror; for just a few hours afterward, I had become a strawberry blonde! But as the months passed and my hair grew out . . . "Eeew! Dark roots!" Then the roots became equal in measure to my blonde hair. It was a scary looking sight; take my word for it. I wore bandanas to school lots of days to hide the mess.

Summer had passed, and I didn't know any other economical solution, but to have my Aunt Jean cut the blonde part of my hair off.

When she did, it was as if I had been made a whole new person! I felt beautiful! It was so amazing to me how a hairdresser could change someone's confidence and outlook with just a snip or two of the scissors. Now, with the opportunity at hand, I just had to be like my Aunt Jean; so off to Alamance Beauty College I went. It was February 1984.

While at Beauty School, I met lots of people that were like me. They wanted to make a difference too, it seemed. I wanted to be friends with them *all*. Another student and I used to get picked on about being the Teacher's Pets, because Miss Lanier would often call on us to take over doing a new style or procedure we were learning, after she had demonstrated it. But to me, it was frightening! "What if we mess up in front of the whole class?" I'd be thinking. Most times though, all went well, and Tracy and I were more confident in the end for it.

Although all was going well at A.B.C., I still had not forgotten my yearning for a child. I asked Matt when we could start a family. He knew what emotional scars the abortion had left on me, so he lovingly gave into my pleadings.

The first month trying to get pregnant, I was so hopeful that my period wouldn't come. It did anyway. The next month's results were the very same. I began to have this really strong doubt that God would allow me another chance to be a mother. And with each "time of the month" that came and went, I knew that He was right to judge me so.

There was another girl in my class that wanted to get pregnant also. I remember the last 2 months of trying, Phyllis and I were going to the doctor for our tests. Urine tests had come back negative on me several times, and she had the same unwanted news to share with me, but I had been having symptoms of being pregnant even with the negative results on the tests. I had heard that blood tests were more accurate, and both of us went for one. They do not get the readings right away on those, so a few days later; both Phyllis and I stood at the payphone inside at the beauty college and made the calls. The results: We both were going to be mothers! When I received my answer, I put on a Maternity blouse and went to tell my husband the wonderful news at work. He was pleasantly surprised!

All through Cosmetology School, I carried this "extra person"; "My second chance" inside of me. I had a few cravings as usual, but I mostly just wanted Taco Bell food. The running joke at school was, "Who wants to go with LuAnn TODAY to Taco Bell for lunch?" They had to switch off with each other to satisfy the hunger of this pregnant woman they called their friend, because not ONE of them wanted Taco Bell *everyday*.

I graduated from Alamance Beauty College in February of 1985 with huge belly and "A"s as my final scores. I studied at home after that for the State Board Exam. They gave me a specific date in April that I was to be at an appointed location for that exam.

My due date was late March, and we were now already into April. No baby yet. I began to have thoughts again of God's Judgment on me for what I had so carelessly and thoughtlessly done to my first child. It crossed my mind several times, that God may have my 2nd child be born on my 1st child's abortion date, or worse yet, take him from me . . . not allowing him to live at all. Still, I knew that God would have been Just in doing so.

But on April 11, 1985, after 15 ½ hours of labor and a doctor shift change, our son, David Joshua Tucker was born.

And by the way, I did not make it to the State Board for that first date they had given me, because I was in the hospital having our baby!

However, I went to the "Board" for my exam a month later, and I became a New Mom and New Hairdresser just like that.

It would not be until years later, that I would learn about the words that fit this chapter perfectly: They are:

Mercy = Not receiving punishment that I absolutely *do* deserve

Grace = Receiving something wonderful that I absolutely *do not* deserve

Chapter Nine

Linda

This is my commandment, That ye love one another, as I have loved you. John 15:12

Now that I had a Cosmetology License and a newborn, I definitely needed to go to work and earn some money! So just past the "6 week period" of healing after childbirth, I stepped right into the Hairdresser workforce. I was hired as a Cosmetologist by Regis Hair Salon located in the Holly Hill Mall, Burlington. Nervous about my first day on the job, as most people are; I felt I wasn't as cool and confident as before my pregnancy because I'd put on about 50 lbs.

Trying my very best to fit in, just did not "do the trick" for the hyper and hip, pushy boss I was placed under. He yelled and pitched fits when his workers didn't do what he thought they ought to have done. His verbal abuse beat me further into my "worthless" state of mind, and to the point I wanted to cower in a corner. I didn't stay long there, but I didn't leave without reporting him to his superiors. They placed someone else into his position almost immediately and I was contacted and told that I could come back there to work anytime I wanted to.

After that experience, though, I chose to apply and work at a small salon, at Cum Park Plaza, near our home. There were only 4 or 5 employees at *this* Shop, but I learned a lot from them. After a few months there, business started to slow for all of us, so I began to watch the Classifieds for openings in the same field. My desire was to be a tad busier and to make more money.

One day, the ad I had been looking for was there. *Hairdresser Wanted for a two booth salon. Gibsonville. Booth rent $25 a week.* I called the number the ad provided and went to meet the owner and operator of Linda's Beauty Salon. Linda Rumple talked with me about the 'open booth' she desired to fill. I asked *her* questions and she asked *me* questions. Somehow, we just knew, we would work together well. And work well, we did.

You see, Linda knew how it was to be a new mom. She had 2 girls of her own. She loved to do hair too, and I think she would have stayed in that shop 24/7 if she had not needed to tend to the needs of her family. Even on her longest days at the Shop, if someone called and needed an emergency haircut for a trip or special event, she would say, "Well, if you can be here by such-n-such time, I will squeeze you in." But hairdressing *wasn't* Linda's "First Love". You see, Linda had someone in her life that, well, GAVE her Life. She was able to share that contagious smile of hers, because this friend had smiled on her. She said His name was JESUS.

From the moment I walked into her Salon the first day, Linda looked at me through special eyes. She saw me where I was: I was overweight, a smoker, (probably still cussed), a new mother, and a "green" hairdresser". But, Linda also saw me where I *should* and WOULD be going. She saw what the LORD *could* do with me. She focused on the goodness instead of the "not so good".

While I was working at her Salon, Linda introduced me to her family. I met her girls, Carrie and Jodie, husband Don, and eventually her Dad, Mom and siblings. Her family treated me, my husband and Joshua like we were blood relatives! They invited us to church, shared meals with us, and continually spoke kind and encouraging words. My husband did not go to church many times with me, but I found several people there that had the same kind of "light" coming from them as my friend Linda had. I wanted that same "positive" and "soothing" gentleness to be a part of me and my family too. The folks at the First Church of the Nazarene reminded me that it was JESUS inside their heart, and in their lives, that made the difference. I was so glad that Linda had shared her church and family with me.

Back at the "Shop", Linda and I had many memorable times together. If one of us laughed, the other would follow. If one cried, the other was right by their side. Even when my husband and I were having marital problems that I could not share with just anyone, Linda was my confidant. She was a compassionate listener and always pointed me to JESUS for the Ultimate Answer.

When we found that I was going to be a "mama" again, she was there to help me be a good mother to my unborn baby. With her continuous encouragement and the Lord's, I was able to quit smoking as soon as I found I was pregnant, for I had restarted that bad habit after my first child was born. She reminded me how important good nutrition was for the baby I was carrying also. I remember eating an apple a day along with other "good for you" foods with my unborn child in mind. I even took a helping of "Green Beans", when offered, although I reeeeaallllly disliked the taste of them—just to help my baby to be healthy. When that sweet little Mary Kathrine Tucker was born on February 28, 1987, she weighed 7 lbs. and 15 ounces. We then named Linda as her "Godmother".

Some time early the next year, my Dad and Mom chose to bless my siblings and I with a gift of a down payment on our houses. We were so excited to have a chance to put our families into homes we could call our own. This choice my parents had made brought on a pleasant time in our lives, but sometimes, there are choices that have to be made that are not quite so pleasant. These choices are hard and at times very hurtful; ones you sometimes think you may never get past.

I was grateful for the unearned gift of a new start in a home, but this was one of those times I spoke of. For my parents knew that my husband and I weren't making enough money between us to make a house payment, so I had to choose: my job at Linda's Beauty Salon, or this home for my family. It was not an easy decision. I chose our home. My parents explained that I would need to work a fulltime job with benefits, and not in a Salon where my income was up and down. I soon after, applied at SCI Systems, Inc. of Graham, N.C.

Leaving Linda, and going to work at SCI was a major "switch off". I went from working with one person to 300 people, from working 4 days to 5 or 6, and yes, I made lots more money for our family. I enjoyed working at SCI most days. As a matter of fact, I succeed greatly at everything I put my hand to. (And we know now that it was only the Lord's doings) But I missed Linda and the smell of her special "Fireside Coffee" brewing in the shop. I missed walking down the street to the florist and bringing her pretty pink carnations on one of her "not so good" days. I missed her laughter and the peacefulness of her voice. I missed the look of JESUS in her eyes.

Linda and I kept in touch here and there. I stopped going to church, using the excuse of being so tired from work and the fact that my husband wouldn't go with me. It was so much easier to stay home.

I eventually got a divorce and move to Virginia. (that's another chapter) While I was there, though, Linda was diagnosed with the rare disease: Amyloidosis. The few times I came to visit, she was weak physically, but still oh so strong in the LORD. She witnessed to people in and out of the hospitals she frequented. She used every opportunity to share God's Love. Linda died on June 12, 1997 at 49 years of age.

Linda was able to give away a pure and special love to others, because her JESUS gave her that Love First. She showed me what it was like *to love* and *to be loved* by the One True Living God, our LORD and Savior JESUS CHRIST.

God cannot give us a happiness and peace

apart from Himself, because it is not there.

There is no such thing.

C.S. Lewis

Chapter Ten

Back To "The Old Way"
With Two To Tag Along

Because thou hast forgotten the God of thy salvation, and hast not been mindful of the rock of they strength, therefore shalt thou plant pleasant plants, and shalt set it with strange slips: In the day shalt thou make thy plant to grow, and in the morning shalt thou make thy seed to flourish: but the harvest shall be a heap in the day of grief and of desperate sorrow. Isaiah 17:10-11

As I mentioned in the last chapter, Matt and I divorced. Joshua was 3 and Kathy, a year old, when we moved into our home. It was located at 1333 Cloverdale Street in Burlington. I had not wanted to leave their Daddy, but problems we were having were not being resolved and the children were suffering. I knew it would affect them throughout their lives if it continued. I was not a perfect wife or mother, but I loved my children and truly believed that leaving was the only way to protect them.

I was having those issues again about trusting people. But this time it was different. I had my children to think about. I couldn't just be "full of hate" and "self destructive" again. I tried to keep the hurt inside from my little ones during the day. The only time I felt I was not strong enough to "keep going" was after I put them to bed in the evening. And although I tried to be quiet when I went to my own room, my son used to overhear me crying in my bed, because I missed and wanted to be with his daddy.

Hearing his "mother's" quiet tears, Joshua would come to my room, and crawl up in the bed with me. With his tiny 3 year old hand, he would pat my arm soothingly, and whisper, "It'w be awight, mommy. It'w be awight."

I worked hard at SCI; every chance I got to learn a new position, I took it. And since I "worked very hard" Monday through Friday, I felt at liberty to "play very hard" on Saturday and Sunday.

Beginning each Friday evening, I would have a babysitter stay with the children and go drinking and dancing with friends. Party! Party! Party! Anything to forget the past and numb the hurt. I was so determined to get out of the house each weekend that I remember getting angry the times my department at SCI was scheduled to work on Saturdays, because that meant, I couldn't go out on Friday evening. (I'd tried that before; working with a hangover; it wasn't the most pleasant thing)

The times I was able to go though, I made the best of it. There were lots of men that bought me drinks, but the bartender was the one that had me try the 'new drinks' he was just learning to make; for FREE. I *did* go home alone each night, but I had plenty of dates that stemmed from socializing there.

One day, while I was at work, I was called to the guard's office to take a phone call. The young woman on the other end of the line seemed cautious and chose her words carefully. She told me that she was an acquaintance of a man I had dated several times. She told me that this man had indeed, tested Positive for HIV. As I listened to her words intently, and quizzed her on her facts, she shared that she, too, had to be tested. She advised that I needed to go soon, to know if I was infected.

I don't know how I got back to my station that day, or how I finished my shift, but I knew what I had to do.

Reality was quickly making way into my "take and do what I want" world. Suddenly, this "Mack-truck" kind of "unwanted news" brought my unorganized, self-serving life to an immediate halt.

This young woman, we'll call Becky, had given me her number, so that I could call her after work. I used that number to reach out to the only person I could talk to in this situation. Becky took my call that afternoon, and offered to go with me to the Alamance County Health Department to get the test. Because I had accepted her offer, I met her the next day at the Family Business she ran. There, she introduced me to her mother and sister. I was shocked when they told me how sorry they were, and asked if they could pray for me before I left. They joined hands in a circle with me, and did just that. They asked their Father to take care of me and allow me to live out my life, free of this deadly disease. I thanked and hugged them for their kindness and looked at Becky, as a signal I was ready to go.

Becky drove me to the clinic afterward. She sat patiently with me in the waiting room but allowed me to go to the back alone; she was there for me when I had no one else. It was well known, at that time, if one received the results of : HIV Positive, it was like handing that person a death sentence. There were little if any medications for this newly discovered disease. I had surely brought this upon myself, through my irresponsible and careless living.

As Becky dropped me back off at my car, I knew it would be 3 days before the results of the HIV test would be ready. That gave me just enough time to spend seeking the One that I should have been looking to and longing for all along.

Sitting in my car, in the Roses Department Store Parking Lot, where Becky had dropped me off, I realized that if I were to have HIV and die, I would be leaving two little ones, without a mom. I would be leaving behind two little ones that could not be raised by their Dad at that time. "How could I have been so careless and selfish?" I said to myself.

Left to right: Joshua, LuAnn, Kathy

Then I began to plead desperately for my life. I told God that I was sorry for the way I had been living. And although I knew I had no right to; I asked Him for one more chance. I promised Him that I would not be frivolous with the time He gave me here. Knowing my fate was in His Hands, I cried and continued, "Please, LORD, just let me raise Joshua and Kathy. I will make sure they know *Who* You are and the *Love* You have to offer. Please, LORD, Please; let me live."

The next 3 days were torturous, but I needed every bit of those 72 hours to THINK ABOUT what a BIG DEAL this was. Something needed to change; and soon.

Chapter Eleven

Settling Down

When Jesus had lifted up himself, and saw none but the woman, he said unto her, Woman, where are those thine accusers? Hath no man condemned thee? She said, No man, Lord. And Jesus said unto her, Neither do I condemn thee: go, and sin no more. John 8:10

Fast forward to Summer of 1989. 'Rocky' and 'uphill' starts are always the best, because after that, it all seems like smooth sailing!

I had a rough beginning, desiring to keep my promise to God. I tried to stay away from the "night club" I'd been frequenting for so long. I broke up with a guard I had been dating from SCI. I told him I couldn't play games anymore. Not long after that I met some body builder. His looks impressed me, but his attitude and temper were a little too much to handle. I think he wanted me *and* my sister. I told him it was over not long after our relationship began.

One warm summer evening, I was walking down my driveway; Yes, still on Cloverdale Street. As the sound of granite rocks ground beneath my tennis shoes, I began talking to the Lord; just letting Him know how I'd been feeling that day. "I'm so tired." "What is wrong with me, LORD?", "Why can't I do this right?" "Please, Lord, help me. Please. I need You to show me how to do this . . . which way to go, I mean. I'm so tired of me and my ways." As I walked slowly back up to the house, I was hoping He had heard me.

Staying busy at work, I learned as much as I could. People sometimes complained about our company not paying a competitive wage for the kind of work we did. After all, we *were* in the business of building Printed Circuit Boards and Computers for big named companies. I may have agreed silently with them and their complaints, but I knew if I kept learning, that I was actually getting FREE instruction; on the job training, so-to-speak. I felt that *I* was taking advantage of *the company* not the other way around!

One day, when I was packing and transporting IBM computers to the warehouse on skids, I noticed that one of the technicians was paying more attention to me than usual. I figured it was just because I had seen him at Burlington City Park with his little girl the Saturday before. We began to talk more and more at work, and he asked me to go with him on a date.

I played pretty hard-to-get when he pursued me at work, because at that point, I felt like I didn't need anyone. I was trying to be good; trying to be patient and wait on God. Some of the girls told me I was crazy for putting him off, but I wanted him to know that I wasn't some "easy girl" that he could just take out and get drunk, and take advantage of.

My display of being "not so desperate" paid off. When I *did* say "Yes" to a date with Mike, he treated me with respect. He took me to nice restaurants, for drives and picnics in the mountains, just to observe the beautiful view. When I began getting to know him, I found out that his wife had left him with quite a bit of debt and that she had also taken his daughter with her; the one I had seen at the Park. It was a very sad story. Mike was trying to put his life back together both emotionally and financially. His life seemed to be at its lowest low when I met him. He had little money, he missed his daughter, and he lived in a small apartment 30 miles away from her; for he'd had to sell the house in Greensboro they'd had together. His mother had helped him furnish his new place with necessity items. I found myself wanting to help him too.

Mike and I seemed to be good for each other. I enjoyed being with him; we both had just enough intellect to make conversations interesting. His daughter, Kayla was 3 years old and *my* daughter, Kathy was also.

We planned outings with our children together. He had so many stories from his childhood to share; he kept me in stitches constantly.

In March of 1990, Mike was sent on a business trip to the SCI Plant in Carlsbad, California to work on some of their equipment. Nearing the end of his one-week-stay, his boss informed him by phone that he had to remain for another week. Back at the plant in Graham, I was part of a department that was working sporadic hours because of shortages. Some weeks, we were off, other weeks we'd work only 24 hours. So, when Mike told me the bad news about his extended stay in Carlsbad, over the phone, I came up with a plan.

I had already filed my 1989 tax information for the previous year. In my estimations, I would be receiving a refund of over $1,000. I talked to a couple of people and my Grandma Horner about loaning me a portion of that money, to buy a ticket to California, which would enable me to spend a few days with Mike there. I figured that this SCI Plant on the west coast may allow me to work while Mike did. It was better than sitting at home, right?

I talked with my Supervisor about it. He wasn't too keen on the idea, but could not guarantee me hours there at the Graham plant, so I left and caught a ride on my first "Airliner Flight" EVER ! All 3 people had come through on the loans which had enabled me to go!

While I was in California, I worked each day at their SCI Plant. Mike and I would lounge by the pool afterwards, in mild, but sunny, upper 70 degree weather. As I looked around at the beautiful and unusual scenery surrounding me, it astonished me so, to know that I was actually in the state of California!

On the last day we worked there, the Plant Manager called me in the office and told me that some folks at SCI, Graham were attempting to terminate my employment. He made arrangements for a conference call with the Head of my home plant. There was some 'touch and go' moments during that call, but I found that SCI, Carlsbad, was definitely on my side. The Head Manager there had actually been in our plant in Graham several times. He remembered me from there. I left that day, knowing that I had a good chance at being able to keep my job in Graham. It was a frightful time, but I remember Mike holding my hand as we walked away from the Carlsbad Plant and down its sidewalk, "If they fire you when we get back home, don't worry, LuAnn. I'll take care of you and the kids until you can find another job." At that moment, I believed him, and began to know how he really felt about me. I was able to keep my job upon return, pay back the loans of my trusting friends and Grandma and had some awesome memories stored for the duration.

Two months had passed since the "job scare", and all was back to normal at home. Mike had gone to visit his Mother in Tennessee on "Mother's Day Weekend". He and his mom liked to go to yard sales together when the weather was nice, so when Mike told me that he had brought something back upon his return, I naturally assumed it was a second hand shirt or candle; something simple. He called me from my yard work over to his bright red truck he'd pulled in the driveway. I was thinking, "It must be something too large to carry, because he called me over to the truck instead of hiding it behind his back." Closing my eyes tight, as he requested, I waited for the surprise of an old sewing machine or bicycle, but when I opened them, I saw before my face, a beautiful diamond engagement ring. He asked me if I would be his wife. But just like before, when I'd hesitated on dating him, I didn't take the ring until he answered a question for me: "Do you believe in God?" I waited cautiously for his response. Mike answered, "Yes, LuAnn, I do!" Again, with hesitation, I said, "You know if you marry me, you'll be marrying my children too . . ." I trailed off, thinking, "Here's your chance to back out buddy." His response was, "Don't you think I've thought about that LuAnn?" And I could find not another thing to say accept, "Yes! I will be your wife!"

On October 6, 1990, one year after we had begun dating, Mike and I were married. Besides saying "I do", there are three things I remember most about our Wedding that took place outside our home: One: Joshua and Kathy had just gotten over chicken pox and the dots were still on their poor little faces at that day. Two: A stray kitten came out of nowhere and pulled at the strings of my bouquet during the ceremony.

Three: Mike had given me a dozen red roses just the day before (one rose for each month we had dated) and since we were leaving for our honeymoon right after the ceremony, we gave away the roses; one to each woman present that day.

It was quite a day to remember. And for one of my guests, it would be the last special gathering she would be able to attend.

Chapter Twelve

The Taste Of Gratitude

I called upon the LORD in distress:
the LORD answered me, and set me in a large
place. Psalm 118:5

The next 4 years were full of hours at work, trips to Tennessee, spending time with family and new experiences.

Time seemed to rush by because of our busy schedules. One of those "new experiences" I spoke of was "Biking". Mike knew that I loved any chance to ride a motorcycle. When we were dating, I had rented one for 24 hours for his birthday. He had owned bikes since he was 9 or so and had sold his last one before we'd met.

While we were married, however, he found a used Yamaha V-Max in the classifieds and purchased it for us to ride. I enjoyed the freedom I felt while the air rushed around us as we flew! There was just nothing that compared it to.

Ever since I was in the 8th grade, and had secretly ridden a motorcycle with a young man from the YMCA, I had admired them and their riders. Inside, I had the desire to BE one of those riders . . . I mean to have one of my own!

One day during the spring, Mike found out about a 1982 Yamaha Maxim that was for sale somewhere in Tennessee. He took his big red truck, made a quick visit with his Mom and Brother, and picked it up. The excitement and tears in my eyes when he pulled into the driveway told him how much joy he'd brought to me. But then there was the task of teaching me to "drive" the thing. At first, I wondered how in the world I could possibly take a chance of wrecking this one owner, nail polish red, perfect beauty of a bike. But I knew the satisfaction of knowing how to ride, in the end, would far out weigh that risk. With much encouragement and training, the day had finally come when I pulled into my Dad and Mom's driveway with Mike and announced, "I'm a biker!" Dad just laughed while Mom asked, "Have you lost your ever-lovin' mind?" I couldn't wipe the grin off of my face for at least 24 hours!

There were so many great moments shared, whether we were on our bikes or off. Times were good. But there is a balance we must acknowledge in life; where there is *good*, *bad* is right around the next corner. Hence: You must take the bad with the good.

Working at the same facility had its challenges for husband and wife. When we got married, Mike and I were required to work in different departments. But after the initial move from my department, once again, I found it as a challenge to increase my knowledge and skills. Throwing myself into work, I excelled. The Lord blessed me greatly. Promoted to "Utility Operator", I would put 50-60 hours in a week at times. On the mornings I chose to punch in at 3am to ready the department for 1st shift's arrival, Mike would take the children to our "sitter's" home, and she then transported them to school at the appropriate time.

I worked a busy week, but some weekends, I would visit my Grandma Horner in a local nursing home where she had been placed after her diagnosis of Alzheimer's. While there, I would shampoo her hair and style it for her. She was a finely primped little lady and loved to look her best.

Circumstances at work began to change and through some shortages of contracts, layoffs began to take place at SCI. With the skills I had "hoarded up", I knew there was little threat for me, for even if they got down to a skeleton crew, I knew how to run all machines, build PCB boards and repair them when needed.

While all this was going on, my grandmother got sick and was hospitalized. As she was laying in a bed in ICU, my mother, sister and I stood on either side of her. I remember my mother beginning to sing, "Amazing Grace, how sweet the sound that saved a wretch like me . . ." The song went on as my sister and I joined her singing and then we quietly prayed. I left the hospital and hopped on a motorcycle with my husband. You see, riding in the sun and silence gives you lots of opportunity to think, and to pray. Often, we would just take off and ride with no chosen path or destination. This would be one of those times.

As we approached a stop at the end of a road, there was a sign. "Apex" it said, with an arrow pointing to the left and "Siler City", with an arrow to the right. I knew that my grandmother had grown up in Siler City. Mike and I chose to go to the right and in doing so; we chose the "right direction". I had no idea, that the road would lead us straight to my grandma's childhood home. As we drove by, I noted the time. After stopping to visiting with my Uncle Gyles and Aunt Becky in Siler City, we headed back to Burlington. I found upon our arrival, that my dear grandmother had gone home to be with the LORD. While discussing the details of when she had passed, I found that it was during the very moments we had been passing her old homestead.

Throwing myself back into work, more "troubled times" continued; in one of the testing departments at SCI, there was a young, tall, thin blonde that was known for her part-time modeling experience. I began to be aware that Mike was noticing her more than "the ordinary" quick glance guys perhaps take at such beauty. The more often I saw it, the more anxious I became at work. With the extra load placed on each employee by the present "shortage of workers", plus the constant gnawing of "worry and jealousy" this beautiful girl had provoked in me, I was in constant awareness that I needed a change.

I began to look in the newspaper for job openings in the technical field. I applied at several places.

One day, as I had continued my pursuit of new employment, my eyes fell on an ad in the Classifieds: *"Hairdresser wanted—Alamance Health Care Center"*

I had continued to practice my hairdressing skills through the years; giving perms, color and hair cuts to anyone and everyone that requested them, so when I ran across this invitation, I jumped on it! My heart was racing as I called the number given, to request an interview. The next day, as I drove the short 7 minute drive from my home to AHCC, I looked up and made the statement, "Lord, I really do want this job." and finally, I added, "Grandma, if you have any pull up there, PULL HARD now!" for I did want this job so badly.

Mr. Charles Jackson was his name; yes, the young black man whose smile reminded me of my 3rd grade teacher. We walked the teal and mauve colored halls together as we talked. The beauty shop, located one hall away from the main entrance, was simply done and had 2 booths. My friend Linda *had* to come to mind as I gave it a "once over". Still, as much as my heart longed for the opportunity to serve here, I knew that God had to want it for me, before I could leave SCI.

Each day that passed after the interview, I found it almost impossible to "just stay still". Knowing that Mr. Jackson had more interviews after my own, I tried to be patient and wait for his call. On the 3rd day, I picked up the phone, called and asked for him.

"Hello, Mr. Jackson, this is LuAnn Turner. I was calling to see if you had made your final selection for the facility's hairdresser position . . ." my voice trailed off, pausing for a moment, waiting for his answer. "Why, yes, LuAnn, I was going to call you today. I've been quite busy. I'm glad you called. When is it, LuAnn that you can start?" I almost dropped the phone. "There must be a catch", I thought, waiting for the other shoe to drop. "Oh, yes, Mr. Jackson", I came back to the conversation. "I'll need to give a two weeks notice at work. Is that alright?" "Two weeks from tomorrow, then? That will be great. You'll need to come in sometime before then to do some paperwork for us though." He said. I was ecstatic. "That's great! You want me to come today?" I anxiously replied. "No, no. I'll be leaving here in a bit, but tomorrow or the next day will be fine. That way we'll have everything ready for your first day. Tina will have the paperwork ready for you when you arrive." "Thanks Mr. Jackson. Thank you so much." I don't think I've ever cried to such an extent over one job in all my life. I smiled, imagining that my grandma may have played a small part in this wonderful blessing.

Get this: I could set my own hours and days, be able to take my children to school and pick them up myself. My children's school was only one block from AHCC. This job was a combination of my two "Loves": One was doing hair, the other was "caring for the elderly and handicapped." I was determined to do my very best. I wanted to "give back to the LORD" with gratitude, something, for what He had done for me. From that day forward, at Alamance Health Care Center, I served Him with fervor and quickness! I sought Him for guidance continuously.

Chapter Thirteen

Saying Goodbye To Me

If thou turn away thy foot from the Sabbath, from doing thy pleasure on my holy day; and call the sabbath a delight, the holy of the LORD, honourable; and shalt honour him, not doing thine own ways, nor finding thine own pleasure, nor speaking thine own words: Then shalt thou delight theyself in the LORD; and I will cause thee to ride upon the high places of the earth, and feed thee with the heritage of Jacob thy father: for the mouth of the LORD hath spoken it. Isaiah 58:13-14

The more time I was able to spend with my children, the closer we became. We'd play outside, go to the park, and visit my Grandma's together.

My Grandma Joyce, was a gentle and positive woman. Even with her declining health, which left her in bed alot, she had the brightest outlook on everything. "How are you doing today, Grandma?" I'd ask, as the children gathered round her livingroom bed. "Oh, very well" she'd respond each time. I can still hear the words she spoke so clearly. When I and my siblings were young, she used to make her famous "fried apple pies" for us; and we weren't the only ones that got to enjoy them. If she happened to run out of those sweet melt-in-your-mouth pies, she'd always have a stash of "Fig Newtons" in the storage bin on the side of her stove.

Once, during December, when one of the children were asking Grandma if she was excited about Santa coming to see her, she told them, "Aw. It's been a long time since Santa visited here, honey." We decided to arrange a little visit from Santa for her. She was so surprised. She had given much of her life serving others. It was nice to be able to give back a smidgen of the happiness she'd handed out to so many.

It was only 2 months after my Grandma Horner passed, that my loving and kind Grandma Joyce's heart failed, and she went home to be with the LORD also.

With much heartache and thoughts of where my Grandma's were spending their eternity, I sat around and then laid around for hours, thinking, writing and sketching pictures of them with Jesus. One Sunday, several weeks after Grandma Joyce had left us, Joshua and Kathy came home from one of their many visits to a small local church. A neighborhood family whose children attended school with them had been picking them up to go. I had welcomed the chance to have a little quiet time of my own during their 2 hour excursion.

On this particular Sunday, though, they ran up the driveway and bolted inside the house. "Mama! Mama! We're going to be doing something special next week at church. Can you come with us Mama? Can you come with us?" Their sweet little innocent eyes searched me for "the right answer". "We'll see" I said, knowing it was "a safe one", "We'll see".

Throughout that week, I recalled several times, the question my small ones had asked me. Was I so selfish that I could not give them ONE Sunday, just 2 hours of my time, to satisfy and support their tiny sweet fragile hearts?

The nearer the weekend came, the weaker my excuses seemed to me, as I tossed the idea around in my head. So, on that bright Sunday morning, we hurried around the house, preparing for the ride with the Nortons to the little church on Sandy Cross Road.

Upon arrival, I was able to visit the children's class where Linda, Pastor Walden's wife introduced herself. The children seemed genuinely excited about learning the next lesson she was to teach them. After the short visit, I went on to the main Sanctuary for my own class instruction. During the Sunday school time, I could feel something pricking my heart, as our teacher spoke out of God's Word. When it was time for the 11'oclock service to begin, I remained seated near the back. When the music began to play, again, I felt a hurt inside me. "What is going on?" I questioned myself. "Why are there tears on my face?" The harder I tried to suppress the ache in my chest, the more I jerked and sobbed in pain. "Oh God, I miss You." I whispered. "Look at me now, Lord. I have done so many things wrong. I do not deserve to be loved by You. I am sorry. I'm so sorry."

All through the service, no matter how tight I clinched my jaw or how hard I pinched myself, I could not hold back the tears of repentance that came. It was my time to be healed and whole. It was time to be joined with my Savior once again. I know that there were people that spoke with me that day, but honestly, I remember nothing but the "Clean, Fresh beginning I was granted" by Jesus' Merciful Touch.

Back at home, the first wisdom He gave me came out of my own mouth saying, "Why am I allowing someone else to take my children to learn about the LORD? That is MY job as their parent!" And as quickly as it had escaped past my lips, I was reminded of my desperate promise to the LORD.

So with much jubilation, I began taking my children to Cornerstone Community Church every Sunday. I suddenly was hungry for every word from the BIBLE they would share with me. I felt so complete; so happy.

Some months later, Mike received a job offer from a "Headhunter Group" that matched jobs to people and vice versa. They offered to pay our way out to Virginia, to "check out" the job location that they had matched him with. Mike was a great Technician who could work on the most ancient and most modern of PCB and AI machines. He knew up front that this company would pay big bucks to have him relocate and work for them. The offer was at a Genie Corporation in Shenandoah, Virginia. We took them up on the offer. They generously placed us at the Sheraton; a nice hotel in the nearby city of Harrisonburg. The area was simply beautiful. Surrounded by mountains, this somewhat busy place seemed to invite us into it.

While Mike was on his interview, I searched the phone book in the room for Healthcare facilities. I loved my job and had a desire to do the same kind of work there, if we were to move. I called the numbers listed to inquire. All of the locations already had hairdressers. Surprisingly enough, I was not upset. I knew, in my heart, that if we did move, the LORD would take care of everything. It would surely be an adventure!

Chapter Fourteen

Another Answered Prayer

And he must needs go through Samaria. John 4:4

Sitting at a restaurant one night across from Dad and Mom, Mike began to tell them of the position he had accepted in Virginia. I was listening intently, but also believing I knew what the content of this conversation was to include. As I drizzled the Ranch Dressing onto my salad I listened. "Oh, yes, he is telling them that he's giving his notice at SCI Systems, and that Genie is a great company to go to work for, . . . yes, yes, . . . that me and the children were going to stay here until school was out . . . . What? Me and the children are what?" I was floored! I was confused! I was in shock! As Mike was attempting to finish his story for Dad and Mom, I was looking at him, and tapping his arm and saying, "Um, wait, um, . . . (tapping more) . . . can I hear . . . (still trying to get his attention) . . . that part . . . again . . . um, . . . about . . . ." Finally, I was able to find out the answers to my questions. In front of Dad and Mom, Mike shared his plans . . . "I thought it was best that I go to Virginia first and find a place for us to live, while you stay back here with the children, let them finish their school year and during that time you can also be selling the house." My mind was racing. I could not believe he did not talk to me about this before telling my parents outright, and while sitting at a restaurant dinner table! Suddenly, I felt sick.

When returning home that evening, Mike assured me everything would be alright. He told me that he was going to be making enough money there, that if I only wanted to work part time somewhere in Harrisonburg, that I could, or if I wanted to "not work at all" when we moved; that would be fine too.

Mike finished out his work at SCI, and left for Virginia. The Genie Co. provided a room for him at the same Sheraton we'd stayed in. We were seeing each other on weekends at first, and when Friday's rolled around, I was ready to "get out of the shop" to go see my husband! The very first time I drove the 4 hour trip to see him; I arrived somewhat early and had some time on my hands. I stopped by the local mall in town and walked the long lines of stores in it. While there, I spotted a Christian Book Store. I curiously walked into its large welcoming entrance and immediately heard the sweet sound of an old familiar hymn playing overhead. As I continued through the store, my throat became extremely tight, because I found myself fighting back tears. Why was I crying? Only God knows for sure, but in my heart that day, I felt the same overwhelming power I had experienced back at the Cornerstone Community Church. It must have been the Spirit of God ministering to me. My heart had become so tender again, that just the mention of JESUS' Name sent whirlwinds of gratitude through my being.

I found many things I liked in that Christian Store that day, but I only picked out one to take home. There was a pack of cassette tapes with Children Singing Contemporary Christian Music on them. I wanted to take the opportunity of the 4 hour drive back home, to listen and learn some of these songs. "Perhaps the children will want to learn them too!" I thought.

One Friday just weeks after Mike had begun working for Genie Corp., I was at my job at AHCC anticipating the drive and destination of Harrisonburg. I had my bags packed and in the car for my drive straight from work. Near the end of my workday, however, Mr. Jackson stuck his head in the door of the salon and said, Mike said for you not to leave town. He's coming home." Well I didn't know what was going on. I asked Mr. Jackson, "Did he say why?" He said, "Nope. He just told me to make sure you got the message." I finished the cuts and perms I had on schedule and went home. Later, Mike arrived, as he had said he would, but with his head hanging low.

He tearfully told me that he had just walked out on his job. He went on to say that he couldn't take the pressure at the new position, because at night, he tossed and turned; just could not sleep, and then, he would be at work feeling mentally drained. He sat in the kitchen chair with shoulders slouched and said, "LuAnn, I don't have a job! I have not been without a job since I was 15 years old! What am I supposed to do?" I was trying to be the "Strong one" now, remembering what he'd done for me at SCI, Carlsbad. "Look, honey. It doesn't matter. I still have my job and I can work that one and another one while you stay at home with the children. You can take your time and find "Just the right job" for you, alright? Don't worry!" I prayed for him and asked God to help him through this. "First, I want you to get some rest." I gave him some over-the-counter Pain med with a "PM" on the end of its name, and ran him a hot bath. "And tomorrow, we'll start walking the track together. They say that exercise releases endorphins and that those give you energy and help you feel great! It'll be alright, honey, don't worry."

So there we were. Most folks might think that this was a tragedy, with him loosing his job and all, but I saw it as an opportunity! "Did God not come through for me when I needed another job? Does God not love my Michael too? Just how BIG *is* the God we serve?" I joyfully preached to myself.

I continued praying for Mike. He rested well at night, and walked with me during the day. The weekend passed too quickly for me. It was a time of "closeness" for us. He was not usually a needy man. Mike knew I was praying for him, and I believed that he was hoping this JESUS I'd begun to serve so radically was real, so that he could be at peace with what was going on too.

On Monday, I took the children to school and headed off to work. It was a short day at the shop, and when I returned home, Mike was ecstatic! "LuAnn! LuAnn! They called me!" "Who Mike? Who called you?" I questioned. Mike went onto explain that the man that had hired him at the Genie Plant called and asked him what had happened on Friday. "Did someone say or do something to you? I want to know! We need you out here!" he'd said. Mike explained to him about his insomnia and the man told him to "come back as soon as he was rested up." I was in awe. The LORD had done a quick work for Mike! He had answered our prayers.

Mike was so grateful for what God had done. After the miracle phone call he'd received, he said, "Honey, thank you for praying for me and getting me back to where I was rested and sane again." While facing me, he was holding my hands in his as he spoke. "When we get moved in and all to Virginia, you find us a church out there, and we can go together as a family."

It wasn't long till Mike was packed up and back off to Harrisonburg. (With the PM med in his suitcase, of course) He eventually found a cute little upstairs apartment in town and our weekend visits continued.

The LORD began to reveal to me, more and more of the things I needed to change in my life while we waited for summer to arrive. Sometimes, He'd let me see it in someone else, and then show me how He saw that very thing in me.

While attending church one Sunday, as we made our way to our car after service, I noticed a couple of folks smoking in the parking lot. I actually was a "smoker" myself, but something about this picture did not look right. I asked the LORD what it was. He let me in on how our bodies are Temples of the Holy Spirit. I knew that it was time for me to get rid of my 16 year cigarette habit and dependence. When my heart had been "readied" He then showed me the way out. And believe it or not . . . it was painless!

I was to begin on the first day, with the most cigarettes I'd ever smoked in a 24 hour period. I began with 20 cigarettes. (That's one whole pack) I used a cigarette pack with a flip top box. I marked a "20" on the lid of it. I smoked from that package that first day, all that I wanted. The next day, I took a different pack and marked it with a "19". I was allowed that many for that day. Each day, I marked one number less and put that many cigarettes in the pack. I still felt "in control" for I was able to smoke that number spaced out throughout the day as I pleased, knowing at the *beginning* of the day, how many I had to "last" me. All went smoothly. On the days that I was down to 7, 6, and 5, etc, sometimes I smoked those numbers for 2 or 3 days before I would bump the number down one more notch.

Meanwhile, back on my job as hairdresser at AHCC, the LORD was doing wonders! While there, I passed on the love that Linda had shown me in her salon.

He blessed me; the folks there blessed me. The residents of AHCC looked forward to coming to the shop and knew that they were loved; by JESUS and by me. We all came out winners.

As an extra bonus, while scheduling my own hours, I was able to spend some of my down time with my Aunt Annie Nell. We laughed together a lot. My dad and I had begun spending my lunch breaks together once or twice a week also, going out to the local Western Steak House for their specials. It would be the beginning of a relationship with my Dad that I'd longed for all my life.

LuAnn & Elsie Hunter at AHCC

The months passed quickly that spring and into summer we headed; the house on Cloverdale Street sold, the children finished school and I gave my 2 week notice at work.

It had only been one year since I'd begun my employment at AHCC, but during that year, the LORD enabled me to join with many others, who each day, made a difference in people's lives. I was also blessed to meet those few precious folks that had, while there, passed from this life into the next. At times I envied them, knowing that as each one left *my* presence; they were just a moment afterwards, able to see JESUS face to face. I often pondered just how it would feel to be where they were.

Working at Alamance Health Care Center had been the favorite job of my 17 years in the "workforce". "Reality" far surpassed my "vision" for the teal and mauve decorated room I'd seen my first day there. As I closed the door to the shop for the last time, I knew I had completed what I'd been there to experience, to learn and to do.

I believe in Christianity as I believe that

the sun has risen:

Not only because I see it, but because by it

I see everything else.

C.S. Lewis

Chapter Fifteen

Who Me?

I will lift up mine eyes unto the hills, from whence cometh my help. My help cometh from the LORD, which made heaven and earth. Psalm 121:1-2

The house on Cloverdale had sold and Mike, Joshua, Kathy and I moved in July 1995, to a home that fit our family perfectly.

The Lord had even taken away my dependency on cigarettes. By the time we had moved to Harrisonburg, I was down to 2 smokes a day. I even remember when Day One came. I would smoke ½ the cigarette in the morning after breakfast, and the other ½ that evening after dinner. I left a pack of cigarettes in a kitchen drawer after I'd quit, just to remind me, that it was *my choice* each day to not have one.

Only one week after our move we found the church we were to attend. How did we come upon it, you ask? I looked in the Yellow Pages! Well, what would YOU do in a place where you knew no one? I have to admit, there was a tad more effort placed in it than that. I prayed to the Lord and then asked myself, "What church have I learned the most about Jesus, His ways and His Love in? It was the Nazarene Church that Linda had brought us to! So that's where we began attending: The Harrisonburg First Church Of The Nazarene.

During the transition from living all my life around family and friends I had grown up with, to being suddenly in this place where I knew no one, took some "getting used to". Mike was gone till 4 or 5 each day, and when he got home, he'd need some "down time" to unwind. He'd been around loud machines and people all day. On the other hand, I had been busy with "readying" the house, tending to children and in need myself of an adult to chat with. Mike was usually too tired to do the "chatting" thing, so I became more and more dependant on God to be my listener.

Some nights, when the stars would be visible, and shining up in the sky, I would sit out on our front steps and talk to the Lord. I remember one particular night, when the crickets were extra chirpy and the moon was shining to its fullest, I told Him, "You brought us here, and I know You'll continue to take care of us." Yes, from the time I'd heard, way back in March, of "the move" we were to make, I knew with every fiber in my being, "*God Has Big Plans For Us*". And I was at peace in my heart with His Plans. He'd even prepared us to fit right into the Nazarene Church there; for from the very first Sunday, we found that the songs we'd learned from those cassette tapes I'd purchased, were exactly what their congregation was singing.

Eventually I began to look for employment, since my phonebook search had not panned out too well prior to our move to Harrisonburg. (Don't you just love those Yellow Pages?) There was no way I could sit at home all the time. But there was so much to do when we first moved. I stayed busy unpacking boxes, treating the basement walls, refinishing and filling in under the deck, and putting rock around everything that didn't move, outside. So, with all of those tasks completed, and after the children had started at their new school, I knew it was time to search for my first job in Virginia. Checking once again at all the Healthcare Facilities for Hairdressing jobs, I found nothing. I began to read the Medical section again under Help Wanted in the newspaper. Shortly after that, I saw an ad for "Activities Assistant". I called the facility named and went for an interview with Jill Siegel.

She was a tall, energetic, caring young woman that cut right to the chase. So, after my interview and hire, I showed up for my first day as an employee at Avante'. Jill explained to me in more detail, my daily duties there. I was to "Put Annie's pill down her throat, read the newspaper to, and play games with, and write letters for, the residents; make sure to document all in attendance . . . oh, and clean the bird cage once a week".

"Okay", I replied, "But just one thing, . . . who is Annie ?". "Oh", Jill said, frankly, "She's the resident "Boxer bulldog." "Ooo-kaaay", I hesitantly let out, wondering if it was too late to make a run for the door.

Do you think I wanted to just walk into this "great challenge-of-a-job" that included "sticking my finger down a big dog's throat, that doesn't even know me?" Well . . . NO! I didn't! But you know; I knew who was in control. I knew who brought me to Harrisonburg, I knew who loved me, and I knew who would help me do all these things the way my boss wanted them done. Besides, Jill showed me a trick to sticking that pill down Annie's throat!

About 8 months had passed since my first day with Jill. The dog and I had become quite chummy. I had gotten to know the residents fairly well and cared about them as individuals. As I read the newspaper to them each morning, several of them would laughingly correct me as I mispronounced their surrounding towns and last names in the obituary. Well, how would YOU pronounce "Staunton, Massanutten, Weyers Cave and Knepper"? See? That's what I thought.

Most days, while I was in our little closet-of-an-office to do my "paperwork", I would leave the door cracked. It wasn't just to get some fresh air in the room; it was so that I could hear some of the '20 minute devotional' that Avante's Chaplin Bob was sharing with the folks there. One afternoon, just after I'd gathered the residents together for the *Bible Study with Chaplin Bob*, I overheard an unusual bit of news. After running through a quick 10 minute story, Chaplin Bob began to share with the residents in attendance that he had been asked to Pastor a church. He explained to his little gathering that day, that he loved all of them, and also had enjoyed working for Avante. He told them, "I have been waiting for this opportunity a long time". I had completely stopped all charting at that point, in order to pay closer attention, still listening through the doorway. His voice was careful and steady, professionally delivering the facts without provocation or inept emotion.

The residents seemed to accept the news. As I glanced through the opened door, I noticed that some looked disappointed while others expressed their happiness for him.

When my boss, Jill squeezed into the office and sat in the chair next to mine, I inquired of Chaplin Bob's leaving. She said, "Oh, yea", in a sad voice. "And they're not going to replace him either." She added. "What?" I asked. "Why not?" Jill went on to explain that the company decided when Chaplin Bob gave his notice, that they would just cut it out of the budget altogether. "Aw. No Way! That's terrible!" I sympathized. "What are the residents going to do without a Chaplin, Jill?" "I don't know. I guess some may have a pastor that can help them if they need it." She hesitantly rationalized, acting as if she really didn't believe her own statement. Then she expressed her doubts, "But most don't get visited by their ministers anymore." My mouth was wide opened in disbelief. "What are they supposed to do if they are sick and need prayer? What are they to do if they have a question about God's Word? And how are they supposed to keep studying and remember that Jesus loves them, if they don't have a Chaplin here?" My voice was pleading. I wondered if I was caring a little too much to be just a peon of a part-time employee. After all, I was not a "Bigwig" in the company; and I was certainly not a family member or resident. "I don't know, LuAnn. They need a Chaplin, but what can we do? They make the rules." Jill ended sadly.

I heard Chaplin Bob closing his "little talk" with the folks in the room next to us, so I scooted my chair back and opened the once cracked door, stepped out and assisted the residents to their rooms.

When I returned, I had not shaken off the "report" of the "Soon to be absent Chaplin". Standing in the activities room just next to the office, I continued my talk with Jill through the doorway. "Jill?" I called softly, just incase she was in the middle of jotting notes. "Yes?" she looked up past the glasses on to the end of her nose. "I was wondering . . ." I stopped again, trying to phrase my words just right . . . "Yes?" she was waiting. I tried to make myself busy with folding a nearby chair. "About the Chaplin leaving . . . Well . . . what if they . . . what if someone was willing to . . . ." I paused. "Are you saying what I think you're saying?" She asked. "Um, well, yes, I guess." I turned around to face her and lifted my lowered head as she spoke. "So you would be willing to do a Bible Study or Devotion with them once or twice each week?" She was grinning now. "Yes. I can try. I mean I might not be too good at it, but someone needs to do it, right?" She was still grinning but had added a nod with it. "But Jill, if you hear of ANYONE else that wants to do it, you let me know, because I'm just saying I'll do it because I don't want them to go without, okay?" "Alright, I'll let you know." She was laughing a bit by that time.

I could not believe I just volunteered to: number one, "get up in front of people" and number two, to talk to them about things in the Bible. I mean, I just got back into church a few months ago myself! What do *I* know? Suddenly I remembered the time I skipped school so that I wouldn't have to stand in front of the class and give a speech.

So, it began, our time together in God's Word. It would be just the beginning of a whole new world for me.

Chapter Sixteen

Trust Me

Though he fall, he shall not be utterly cast down: for the LORD upholdeth him with his hand. I have been young, and now am old; yet have I not seen the righteous forsaken, not his seed begging bread. Psalm 37:24-25

It was fall of 1996. My children, Joshua and Kathy had advanced to 4th and 6th grades. Mike had settled in well into his position at Genie Corp. I had become comfortable with my job and the many facets of it, at Avante'.

One weekend, while we were out to eat, my husband told me about a facility that he had seen on Port Republic Road with a big Satellite Dish out front. He added, "You know, I'll bet they have people that work on PCBs there. You ought to check it out and perhaps apply." I began to ponder the possibilities. You see, when I took the job at Avante', it didn't pay very much an hour, but I wanted to work in that field so badly that I would have taken just about anything they had, to get my foot in the door. Now that I'd been back in the "workforce" for a year since our move, I was curious to what this "City of Harrisonburg" had to offer. "Okay, well, maybe I will, if I have time." I don't know how it affects you, but there's something about the element of surprise that motivates *me*. I'd planned on going to check this place out, but didn't want to let my husband in on it yet.

The following Monday, I drove to the place Mike had seen. I walked in and filled out an application. The tall, older blonde haired lady at the desk was very kind. She answered phones a lot while I was busy writing. "Okay, then" She smiled as I returned the application. "Thank you for applying, and I'm sure they'll let you know if they have anything available." I returned her "thank you and smile" and left. On the drive home, I daydreamed again about what God might have in store.

After climbing the stairs from the basement to the kitchen, I threw my keys on the counter and noticed the answer machine light flashing. Hitting the button: **PLAY**, my eyes widened as I heard: "Yes, this is Jay Moyers calling from Comsonics, Incorporated. I would like to have you come in for an interview at your soonest convenience. Please give me a call at 434-5965 and let us know when you might be able to come. I was shocked! They called me before I could even make it home from Port Road! Wow! Can you imagine me jumping up and down with excitement? I did! Right there in the on the kitchen's shiny linoleum floor! Talk about surprises! Boy, did I have one to tell Mike then! He was as happy as I was about the whole ordeal. So to make a long story short, Comsomics, Inc. hired me, and with a wage that was $ 1.00 more per hour than I was making at Avante'! And that was a lot back then!

Okay. Okay. I know what you're thinking. "What about the residents? What about the Bible Studies?" I was just about to tell you, when you asked. Along with my "notice", I told Jill that I was going to "stay on" as a volunteer, coming in for Bible Studies and to give manicures to the people that wanted one. Isn't the LORD amazing?

I was hired in the fall, as I said, that year. Working still, only 20-30 hours each week, there was plenty of time for Mike and the children, and all the duties of a wife and mother. I was making lots of friends at Comsonics, Inc. and was able to regain my skills and speed at soldering and such.

Just after Christmas that year, our workload lessened, and many of us were assigned odd jobs to keep us busy while fulfilling our normal hours there. I remember loving the variety of assignments. One of my favorites was painting.

It was still early January, and the amount of odd jobs seemed to be dwindling. My boss, one day, called me into his office to talk. Jay let me know that he really did not want to do what he was about to do, but that they were going to have to lay me off. He regretfully looked me in the eye and said, "I'm so sorry LuAnn. We had to let someone go and by the rules, you were last hired and you also are the only Part-time person in this department." He was genuinely sorry; I could tell. It actually surprised me that he was this gentle because he usually gave me a hard time in front of the other girls about how I was *holding* the paintbrush or the *direction* I was *moving* it in. "I promise, LuAnn, I'm going to get you back in here. Just wait a couple of weeks and you'll see. I'm sorry. There was just nothing I could do. The rules state plainly who must go first." I told him that I was okay and thanked him for talking to me about it. "I'll be waiting for your call, Jay." I added, trying not to show my worry.

Driving home that day all kinds of things rolled through my mind.... "I hope he was telling the truth about calling me back in a couple of weeks." "Wow! What projects can I begin and finish in that amount of time?" "Oh, man, Mike's not going to like me being out of work. No work—No money. Nope, He's not going to like this at all."

Our choice of lifestyle had stretched our budget pretty tight at times, but not always. It's not that we lived "High on the Hog" EVER, but we had the normal payments to make, like 2 cars, a house, his child support and all the utilities. The more I thought about it, the more nervous I became about telling him. After all, we'd, just the month before, spent a lot on Christmas gifts for family and friends and for each other.

He always left for work before I did in the mornings, so he didn't know for at least the first week that I was not following my normal routine. I was able to clean out my cluttered car, wash it and take care of a few things not on a weekly schedule. I got busy finding things to do for other people too, so that I could continue to earn money. Some of the girls back at Comsonics must have felt sorry for me, because they asked if I would clean out their cars and wash them like I'd done to mine. They insisted on paying me to do it. One lady even hired me to sit with her handicapped husband a few times, while she went out and ran some errands. Still, what side jobs I had picked up, had not brought in enough to cover the 2 weeks (at least) that I would be out.

To my best recollection, it was the following weekend that I let Mike know what had happened. He expressed his frustration and distrust of the promise my boss had made to me, and left the subject alone after that.

Very early the 2nd week of my "layoff", I decided to 'take on' the challenge of cleaning out the closet in the basement, under the stairs of our home. There had been quite a few boxes and miscellaneous items thrown in there when we first moved. I began by pulling everything out of the tiny space onto the carpeted basement floor. Over an hour had passed as I took a few moments now and then to reminisce of my home and family back in North Carolina, as I looked over some of the items I'd stored. Nearing the last bit of separation and shuffle of the closets contents, I noticed the leather-like black bag that I had carried back and forth, from state to state, while I was visiting Mike during his apartment days. I plopped onto the floor, and while taking a break, ruffled through the items in the bag to see if I needed to put any back into circulation upstairs. After checking the large inner section of the two handled tote, I moved to its side pocket, and wiggled my fingers in. "There seems to be some papers in there." I thought, as I struggled to pull them out of the tight space. "What?" I sat looking at the item in my hand after pulling it out. To my astonishment, and utter amazement what I had thought was folded paper had actually been a subsequent wad of cash!

"Huh?" "What?" "Where did this come from?" I spoke to myself excitedly. By now, I was up on my feet, thumbing threw each bill, counting as I went. "20, 40, 60, 80, 100 . . ." "Oh Lord! There's two hundred dollars here!" My mind went racing back to the times I may have had to have cash of this large amount. Suddenly, I realized, "It was when Mike had insomnia in his first weeks at Genie! I had, at that time, cashed a payroll check and forgotten it was there, in all the turmoil of my husband's brokenness." This money had been in this bag for almost 2 years! And the Lord's timing was perfect, as always. We ended up using the "monetary find" to meet the rest of our normal income, and just as Jay had promised, after 2 weeks, Comsonics called me back to work.

As I wrote in my journal that night; these wonderful workings of the LORD, I ended with, "Thank You, Lord, for knowing and meeting my need, even before I realize I have one. I love You! LuAnn"

Chapter Seventeen

Will You Believe Then?

Howbeit when he, the Spirit of truth, is come, he will guide you into all truth: for he shall not speak of himself; but whatsoever he shall hear, that shall he speak: and he will shew you things to come. John 16:13

After a while, things were back to normal; almost as normal for us as it felt while we were living in North Carolina. Volunteering at Avante' had become a "family affair" and then some. Joshua and Kathy, and sometimes their friends from school, would help out at the weekly Bible Studies, by handing out items, singing and just being loving and kind.

The residents seemed to really enjoy their presence. Numbers of those in attendance of the "get-togethers" increased. We began to have questions and drawings for prizes at the end of each lesson. Their favorite of all the prizes were the Christian T-shirts we'd purchased at a store in North Carolina on visits there. As a matter of fact, 7 years later, when I took another position in Healthcare at another facility, one of the clients rolled in, wearing her t-shirt from all that time ago.

A couple of times, I was asked to fill in for the hairdresser at Avante' while volunteering there. It was easy stepping in to do someone's hair that I already had known for years.

The children and I were learning from and getting more involved with the First Church of the Nazarene. Joshua and Kathy enjoyed being with the young people and I sang in the choir and had started driving a van to pick up children around town and take them to church. Mike said he just didn't want to go to church.

On Wednesday nights before my van route would begin, Mike, the children and I would go out together for dinner at Luigi's. It was an old quant square shaped building with a variety of frilly curtains in the windows and different colored tablecloths. From the looks of it, you really couldn't tell how awesome the Italian Food was inside! Most of those nights, I'd go to choir practice with garlic on my breath and just apologize to the person sitting next to me.

One of those Wednesday nights we ate at Luigis, Mike shared with me some confusion he was having about one of his coworkers. As I sat across from him listening, He complained that this person was constantly mean to him; in his language and in his attitude. He gave some "for instances". After he'd finished, I told Mike that I would pray for him and that man. He balked at my words somewhat. I assured him that the Lord would listen, and hear that prayer. He just smiled and I could tell he had his doubts. "Mike, if I pray for you and this man that you say is mean to you, and the Lord makes things better, will you believe then, that He is real and hears our prayers?" Mike grinned slyly, "Sure, LuAnn, sure. I'll believe then."

We bowed our head right then and there and asked the Lord to tear down the walls that were between the two of them and to please help them to "get along". It wasn't surprising at all to Mike that I took his hand and prayed in a restaurant, because we always said the blessing before we ate, even in this restaurant that had blaring Oldie-Goldie music playing in the background. The children and I went to church as usual that night; Mike went to do his thing, and we met back at home. Nothing else was said that evening about the prayer or his coworker adversary. T.V. and sleep overtook us and the next time I saw my husband was the following afternoon.

"Hey honey" Mike came in the door from downstairs. "What we havin' for supper tonight?" the usual kinds of questions. Then, after a few moments of the "norm", he asked "hey, you know that guy I was telling you about at work? The one that's been so ★#^@★ mean ?" "Yes, I remember . . ." I waited. "Well the funniest thing happened today." Mike busied himself rummaging through the fridge. "And . . . . ?" I was wide eyed by this time. He closed the fridge with a soda in his hand as he continued. "That guy . . . he was so *talkative* to me today." I stayed absolutely still, waiting for more details. He popped the top to his drink, "He was really . . . (trying to find the right words to say) . . . different." "He talked to me like I was his *long time friend*. He acted like he'd never done a thing to piss me off." "Well, so you two are okay now?" I asked. "Yeah, the day went by super fast, 'cause he wasn't actin' like an idiot. I found out a lot about him. Do you know he's got . . . ." The conversation went on, as Mike confirmed what I was sure of all along: God answers prayer.

Chapter Eighteen

December's Distraction

But the Comforter, which is the Holy Ghost, whom the Father will send in my name, he shall teach you all things, and bring all things to your remembrance, whatsoever I have said unto you. John 14:26

The months seemed to fly on. The children went from one grade to the next. I had the opportunity to homeschool them a couple of those years. Schoolwork became an enjoyment instead of a chore. We took outings to special places, adopted a portion of roadway to "keep clean", and Joshua even helped out the youth pastor, at The First Church Of The Nazarene once a week. We had pets and projects that always kept us busy.

One Christmas, Joshua and Kathy's Dad, who lived in Burlington, N.C., asked if he could have them with him during the holidays. I knew the children would like the excitement of the trip and being able to see their relatives living in N.C, so I agreed it would be a great idea. I had never spent a whole Christmas Day and the few surrounding it, away from Joshua and Kathy, so this would be very different for me.

Mike and I stayed busy buying gifts and wrapping them, going out with friends and such, but the children were never far from my thoughts. I asked the LORD to keep them safe, let them have a great time, and to let me not think so obsessively about their absence. What I really needed was a distraction.

One of the projects, or should I say "pet-projects" the children and I enjoyed while homeschooling, was the set of guinea pigs we adopted. It taught the children responsibility, while cleaning out their cage and how to care for living things, placing food and water in for them daily.

An extra bonus we hadn't counted on, however, was that one of the "guineas" got pregnant! When we purchased them, we did not specify for female or male; (for we weren't studying *ANATOMY* yet!)

While Joshua and Kathy were gone, I just added them to the responsibilities of taking care of my other 2 fat, furry friends; our cats, Ki Ki and Buck.

Ki Ki, Buck and Guinea Pigs with LuAnn

Still spending much of the days missing Joshua and Kathy, it was hard scanning their empty rooms as I walked by them while coming down the hall of our home. Each time I passed, I'd utter a quick and quiet prayer: "Help me Lord" and "Keep them safe".

As I woke up Christmas morning, a few days after the children had left; they crossed my mind once again. I looked at the clock and noted that it was time to feed the guinea pigs, so I slipped my bedroom shoes on and shuffled to Kathy's doorway . . .

Rubbing my eyes, as I looked through the glass aquarium,
I thought I must still be asleep;

For what did I see, but a Mama and PaPa Guinea,
With 3 little ones underneath!

With all the joy of a brand new Mother,
I jumped and ran and explained.

Mike was laughing as I told him of the babies,
Then I gave each one of them a name!

What a present for a Christmas morning!
I felt blessed now, no fretting or worry!

And after the gifts the Wisemen had given,
I named them: Goldie, Frankie and Murray.

Chapter Nineteen

He Sees All

And we know that all things work together for good to them that love God, to them who are the called according to his purpose. Romans 8:28

The awesome thing about Harrisonburg, Virginia is, that it's a place surrounded by mountains. Along with its lush green backdrop of scenery, with pinks, reds and white splashes of color in the spring, it is pierced perfectly with streets and highways that are curvy and rolling like decorative ribbons. But this day I'm going to describe to you, is far from picturesque. During the winter months, this bird chirping bright place turns into somewhat of a bad version of Mario Kart at DK Summit on your Wii game.

When it snows in Harrisonburg and its surrounding areas, the VDOT crew are "On it"; like, I mean as of "Yesterday". They usually begin work on the roads the night prior to the nasty weather, and begin early the next morning cleaning up what doesn't melt under their prior "prepping method". It was normal to have schools and businesses open 'on time' when a 3-5" winter blanket had threatened the grounds. On this particular day, things were just as I described. Roads had been cleared, yet we were able to enjoy some beautiful white and glassy scenery during our early commutes.

My usual route to work took me through woods, past cows and farmers fence lines. As I cautiously drove that "way most familiar to me", the roads seemed to be okay. It was just before sunrise when I approached the sharp left banked curve I had expected to be there. I made it around to the straightaway this particular morning, but was surprised to see that the next section of road was a total sheet of ice! In the dim light of the morning, I saw a car with it's flashers on, blinking. I slowed a little to see if someone was in the car, but when I did, my car also began to slide toward the ditch. "Oh, Jesus! Oh Jesus!" I cried out. "Help me!" The car came to a stop right at the edge of the ditch and within just 6 inches from the front of the other car.

I mustered up the courage to get out and walk a bit down the ditch, leaving my flashers on. Within moments, another vehicle came from the same direction and curve that I had, and just like me, they slowed, their vehicle and slid. Just after that one, another vehicle came. After only 10 minutes, there must have been at least 7 vehicles stranded between my car and the beginning of the curve.

Several of us made calls to nonemergency police numbers and VDOT to let them know that we were all out there and how bad that portion of road was. No one could get IN to us from the curve, or OUT from that direction, so we stood around and talked. A couple of us decided to walk down the road a bit as we waited for help. We knew why no one had come from the curve area to assist us, but we had become very curious as to why we hadn't seen any traffic coming from the *opposite* direction.

When we got to the end of the road just before it dropped off, down over a quickly declining steep hill, we stopped, and peered over. Our faces wore the look of SHOCK and our mouths dropped open as we stood speechless. At that moment, we understood the merciful Hand of God; for had we, in our vehicles had not been stopped by the ice in the curve that morning; Had we continued, each one of us, down that road, and reached the place where the hill declined quickly . . . we would have not been able to stop . . . for at the bottom of that hill, stretched an 18 wheeled transfer truck lying on a thick sheet of ice awaiting us.

Failures are finger posts on the road

to achievement.

C.S. Lewis

Chapter Twenty

Do I Stay Or Go?

Be not forgetful to entertain strangers:
for thereby some have entertained angels unawares.
Hebrews 13:2

I had been working at Comsonics, Inc. for quite a while. I had taken a new position as Technician that brought me to the basement of the building. And although I was now on the lower floor, I felt as if I was on top of the world! This position stretched my mind, used that abundance of energy I seemed to have, and gave me a "satisfaction" of accomplishment as I left at the end of each day.

The "station" I was given was located in a room with 4 men. My boss "prepped" them ahead of time, for the new female arrival and made sure they treated me fairly. I enjoyed working with them, because most of the time, they were "all business", and kept to themselves. The language they used sporadically left something to be desired, but I had a CD player with headphones and was allowed to wear it as I worked; That took care of the unwanted bits of conversation for me.

Each summer, after I began to homeschool the children, I would ask Joshua and Kathy if they desired to be homeschooled or attend a Christian School the upcoming year. This particular year, they had chosen Good Shepherd as their source of education. I had been working 50+ hours each week, so that I could have my normal income (based on past part-time work) and the 'extra' to pay the tuition for their schooling. It was challenging in an exciting way, being able to fly through the week, knowing I was working for an eternal cause: the Spiritual Education of my offspring. I often recalled, during the hard-to-get-up mornings, the promise I'd made to the Lord in the Roses Department Store parking lot years before. THAT would give me the incentive I needed to get out of bed. Once I got started, I was fine!

Many people at Comsonics caught onto why I grabbed all the overtime hours that were available. Lots of them shared encouraging words, and like "a runner of a marathon" who was becoming weary in her run, the cheering crowd on the sidelines spurred me on.

Still, I longed for more time with my husband and children and desired having some time at home to do more than just laundry and dishes. Again, I went to the classifieds for a higher paying job.

After a few weeks of persistence, Banta Books called me in for an interview. They were looking for someone for 3rd shift. After the first interview, I had a second. Things were moving fast, and I was getting a little nervous. "Do I really want to leave this job that I know well and love so much?" Then, I would think of my children and husband again. "No More Overtime!" I thought.

But by this time in my life, I was more dependent on God than ever, on decisions to be made. I had been seeking Him about the matter all along. When Banta made me an offer to "come onboard", I asked them for a week to make my decision.

Meanwhile, Mike had scheduled ahead of time, a Daytona Beach Trip for us to celebrate our 10th anniversary which had already passed, but in the cooler months. Now it was summer and he'd invited my Dad and Mom to come along with us and Joshua and Kathy.

While at Daytona Beach, Florida, I shared my "prayer request" with my Mom. She joined me in asking the Lord to show me what I should do.

While enjoying the sunshine and sand of the beach one day, I told my family I was going to take a walk. I had become obsessed with walking during my time working at Comsonics and had done it at least 5 times in each 24 hour period as a routine. But today's walk on the stretch of shoreline was for an entirely different reason. I needed to get alone with the Lord. The time was drawing near, for a final decision to be made for or against Banta. I needed to hear an answer soon.

As I slowly walked along the somewhat crowded length of sand, seagulls cawed and waves overturned onto each other loudly. I thanked

Him for the beautiful picture before me, and then asked Him, "LORD, what is it that *You* would have me do? Time is running out, and I am still on the fence here."

As I looked around at the sunbathers and fellow walkers moving to and fro in a seemingly imaginary line, a woman cut through them on the left and paused at my side. I stopped, thinking I may run into her, and then I heard her speak. She told me with much certainty, that He said, "Go". She mingled back into the crowd just as quickly as she'd come from them. Instantly, the thought ran through my mind, "What just happened? How could this be?" Turning to look for the woman, she'd vanished. I took off rushing to get back to my Mom and told my family what had happened. When I returned home, I obeyed. There was no doubt left in me, as I penned my resignation to Comsonics. He'd come through for me again.

Chapter Twenty-one

Joy Comes In The Morning

Looking unto Jesus the author and finisher of our faith who for the joy that was set before him endured the cross, despising the shame, and is set down at the right hand of the throne of God. Hebrews 12:2

My employer, Comsonics, offered to increase my hourly wage, in hopes it would sway my decision on leaving. It wasn't that I was "that great", but I was an employee they'd taken time to train and mold to their liking. They had an investment in me. But I'm glad they did not offer what Banta was paying because I would have needed to go back to the "drawing board" again, asking the Lord for guidance. I did love my job and only needed more time for my family.

My first week at Banta was filled with paperwork and classes. Each one in attendance seemed a little nervous, as they explained to us some of the dangers in the plant, with the machines. The following week, we "new hires" were scattered among many shifts and departments. I was placed on a "Bindery Line". This "Bindery Line" was run by 5-7 employees.

It was amazing to me how they bound books. I paid close attention to each station the workers on my team filled. Being experienced in running "production lines" I was already imagining the possibilities of what could be learned at this huge place.

A young woman was paired with me as my trainer and began explaining to me what to do: "Clasp your hands firmly onto each stack of books as they make their way down this belt, pick them up as a group and turn them quickly up then down for inspection." I was practicing the "move" as she demonstrated. "The binding should be good quality. No ripples or tears, etc." I looked at an example of "acceptable" and one of "unacceptable" as she continued. "Then, quickly stack them into the box and grab the next "grouping" and do the same." Over and over we practiced, as the clicking and zipping of the machines sounded. It appeared to be an easy job, but one dare not get behind. If the procedure's not done fast enough, the books begin to pile and a mess is the result. My mind went back to the funny yet horrible scene of "I Love Lucy" where she and "Ethel" were working in the chocolate factory.

I was in the best physical shape I'd ever been in and confident that once turned loose, I'd be able to make my boss proud. But for the first night or two, the "trainer", Joy, was to stay by my side. This 5 foot 7 of a female had a somewhat gruff voice that did not seem to match the sweet smile that shone over her face. When dealing with serious matters, her face was still and solemn as if she had a lot on her mind. Her eyes were the prettiest blue, but were dimmed by perhaps strain or chosen lifestyle. While she labored alongside me and with others on our line, a couple of tattoos became visible on her arms.

I was grateful for the tips Joy had given me, and felt somewhat comfortable with her there. Each night, the hours flew quickly by, as our "crew" pushed hard to complete each assignment.

Nearing the end of my first week on the line, I began to have some problems, as my arms and wrist cramped and ached. I'd had sore muscles before with new activities, but this was strangely different. With each night that passed these physical problems became worse and worse.

After my shift ended each morning, I'd go home to soak my forearms and hands. I'd hoped it would decrease the swelling and tightness. I'd had to remove my rings so they wouldn't cut my fingers.

After several nights working, I was only hours from finishing my first week on the floor. The books continued to be forwarded one by one on the belt. As I grabbed each stack of the hard backed books, and flipped them up and down, I could not feel anything on my fingertips, but sharp pains shot through my wrists and arms. I cringed and bit my lip trying not to "cry out" which would have been, to me a sign of weakness.

It was the ending of only my first week at Banta; I didn't know if I could "go on". At 6:30am, the end of the shift, it was nearing sunrise. The lot lights were still on overhead outside. Making my way to the car, I carefully pulled out my keys, opened the door and eased in. Lifting my hands up to place them on the steering wheel, I stopped and laid my head on it instead. Cupping my arms and hands against my body for warmth I began to cry.

"Lord, what is wrong with me?" The star like overhead lights now glistened as I pleaded through my tears. "I need to be able to do this job . . . . And look at me; I can hardly move my arms and wrists. Why is this happening, Lord? I don't understand."

Suddenly, a "Tap, Tap" sounded on my car window. I jumping and took in a quick startled breath. "LuAnn, are you alright in there?" The young woman who'd trained me was right outside my door. "What?" trying to regain my composure, "Yes, I'm okay." I didn't want to worry her with my problems. I didn't want her to see my sad, pathetic state. "Can I get in and sit with you a minute?" she asked. "Well," I paused. "Yes. I guess." I unlocked the other door.

Joy got in the passenger side and closed the door behind her. The morning light was making its way across the Banta lot "Have you been crying, LuAnn?" her gruff voice not sounding as gruff as before. I dropped my head and tightened my jaw, determined not to start up again. "I'm alright", I said. She was not fooled by my short answer. "Tell me, what's wrong?" she persisted gently. I could not fight the tightening of my throat one second longer. As quiet tears made their way down my already salty cheeks, I began to tell of my heart's question. "Before I took this job at Banta, I asked God if I should stay at my old job or come here. He told me to take this job and now, I can't even do it. I just don't know why He brought me here." My unsteady voice trailed off as I looked out the driver's side window, lifting an aching hand to wipe my face.

Joy waited until I'd gained my composure, and began to speak. "LuAnn" she paused "I know why He sent you here." I stopped breathing for a second, thinking I'd misheard what she'd said. "What?" I apologetically asked. "I know why God sent you here, LuAnn." Her blue eyes still looked tired, but different somehow as she finished her confession . . . . "He sent you here for me."

In somewhat disbelief, I asked with hope, "Are you serious?" I laughed and then cried at the same time. "Joy, I don't understand."

Joy had my attention now, but I was not even going to try to interpret her statement. Then she went on to explain. "Remember when we were talking about things the other night while we were working, and on break?" "Yes . . ." I waited. "Well, my grandmother used to teach me about JESUS. I actually got saved when I was little, but my life has been a mess lately." Her tears began to match mine as the heavy drops rolled from her beautiful eyes. I hung onto each word she said, then in finishing she shared, "LuAnn, God sent you here to remind me that He loves me."

Someone could have told me, "You'll never have a job again", at that moment, and it would not have fazed me a bit. The overwhelming presence of the LORD filled the car that morning. And as we joined hands in prayer, and thanked Him for bringing us together, the sun's first ray made its way over the building.

Chapter Twenty-two

What Has He Done To You?

Ye are the salt of the earth: but if the salt have lost his savour, wherewith shall it be salted? it is henceforth good for nothing, but to be cast out, and to be trodden under foot of men. Ye are the light of the world. A city that is set on an hill cannot be hid. Matthew 5:13-14

When I left the lot of Banta that day, I was relieved to know I hadn't failed. Well, yes, in man's eyes, I probably had, but not in my Father's.

Banta's offices were not opened yet, for me to speak with someone about my job, but I knew I had to go on a serious hunt, THAT day, if it was possible, for new employment. "My husband is going to be upset with me." I thought, and "I need to be working." "Look at my arms. Look at my hands. I can hardly move them."

I left work and went straight to Walmart; "Surely, they will have a job for me there" I told myself. I knew it may not be a "career job" for me if I was hired, but it would pay some bills while I continued to search. Back then, their application process was still on paper, and when completed, you could turn it in. With each stroke of my pen, I grimaced as my fingers and wrists turned. I prayed and hoped with all the strength I had left, that they were in need of someone right away.

The recipient of my application, phoned someone in the back to come forward. A young, dark haired man appeared to interview me and we talked for a while. At the end of our serious conversation he asked, "So, how soon can you start?" With a "cheating death grin" on my face I couldn't help but reply, "I can start tonight sir, if that's what you'd like."

I spoke with a lady in Human Resources at Banta of the trouble with my arms. She was very 'understanding' and shared that I had not been the first. She told me that they would like to "keep me on", but the only openings were for "swing shift". Knowing that it would not be good for my family situation; I politely declined, apologized again, and thanked her.

So each night I came into Walmart at 10pm and worked till 7. My wage was somewhat lowered, but in my heart I knew this was just one of those stepping stone opportunities.

The boy Peter, that would be my partner and trainer, couldn't have been more than 18. He had a "tough" outer finish and made out like he cared very little of what people thought of him.

As we tore open each plastic-wrapped grocery pile from the wooden pallets the forklift had delivered to the floor, he explained the ins and outs of the processes our team would follow. With each night that passed, the more confident I became in being a 'help' instead of hindrance to my co-worker. One night, as we loaded shelves side by side, Peter became a bit more verbal than usual. He wasn't having the "best of nights", and as a case of cans spilled opened onto the floor, he used more of the profanities that were in his everyday language.

I looked up from my work and asked in a quiet voice. "Peter, why do you curse at Him like that?" Peter stopped with his hands still on the lids of two cans. "What?" His face appeared distorted. "Um . . . why do you curse the One who made you?" "Are you angry with Him?" I couldn't believe the bold question coming from my lips. I hardly knew this person! But the young man that hadn't seemed to care what people thought before, was now turning red at the suggestion. "No. I'm not mad at Him. I'm just tired of dropping everything I try to pick up . . ." He paused for a couple of seconds. "Sorry", he added. "I guess I could use a little less of the bad language, huh?" He asked. "Well, The Lord's been so good to me. I just wondered what He had done so terrible to deserve you being angry with Him."

Peter then opened up to me like I'd never expected. He shared some things about his separated parents and how he missed spending time with his Dad. We laughed together at some moments and then some others we were just "sad", for the trials he was going through. We talked about the LORD and church for a while. I was reminded of how man looks on the outside, but GOD looks at the heart.

As I continued to work as a Stocker of Groceries at Walmart, I was having some issues of my own. Compared to the income I was expected to "bring in", this less paying job continued to fall short. At times, I would spot someone that I knew as they entered the store. Because I was aware that *they* knew the technical and healthcare background I'd come from, I would cower behind an isle, until they passed by. My pride was getting the best of me. I did not mind, so much the sweat and labor I experienced with this "stockers position", but was somewhat embarrassed of this "new place" the LORD had me in. I prayed many times, asking the LORD, "when will my time here be through?" Each night I'd keep my eyes and ears opened while there, for the spiritual lesson or goal that was to be my final one.

I met many people as I learned how to fill in for absent workers and assist with unloading trucks; they were people from all walks of life, with joys and dreams and troubles similar to my own.

It's true what they say about not really knowing what a person's going through, until you've walked a mile in their shoes. And with each experience the LORD gave me as I knelt along the half full shelves of Walmart, I came to relate to the great and small, who all needed a savior named JESUS.

Chapter Twenty-three

What Do <u>You</u> Love Most?

And God spake all these words, saying, I am the LORD thy God, which have brought thee out of the land of Egypt, out of the house of bondage. Thou shalt have no other gods before me. Exodus 20:1-3

Life continued as I worked for Walmart. Mike threw himself into the Bow Club he'd joined. Joshua and Kathy continued attending Good Shepherd School. The children and I were still involved in church and our weeks had become routine again. The First Church of the Nazarene had built a new church out on Port Republic Road in Harrisonburg, and they were already having problems with seating everyone in their 600 chaired "gymatorium". One solution that the church had chosen to try to resolve this problem, was to increase the morning service from one to two. When they implemented this change, the schedule of services was: Church service, then Sunday School, after that, another Church service; That way all could attend Sunday School together.

As a choir member, you were asked to sing at the beginning of the 1st service, go to Sunday School, then sing again at the beginning of the 2nd service. Some were unable to commit every time, but there were enough of us on each occasion to at least *sound* like a full choir.

I was a tiny thing then, about 117 lbs. I realize some people are thin naturally, but "thin" didn't come that way for me. I watched my weight obsessively and cherished what I did eat, with every bite. So when I did allow myself to enjoy a meal, I shunned the thought of hurrying.

Actually, I would have rather not eaten at all if I had to hurry or if my surroundings were hostile. (ie disagreements going on)

Things were not the best at home in those days and it was difficult to find a common ground to sit and take in nourishment peacefully. So when this two service program began to take effect at church, I constantly found myself very hungry somewhere in the middle.

During our Sunday School Class, (in that middle) they offered coffee and sweets galore. Much of the class time was spent with random socializing, while my mind wandered to "other places". Often times I felt out of sync there; perhaps unsettled inside. It seemed my soul was yearning for MORE of something.

I began to leave church between services, and skip Sunday School altogether. I'd go, sit at a local bagel shop and have a relaxing, peaceful brunch. When I first began this routine of mine, I'd tell Joshua and Kathy to go on to their classes. I'd tell them "I'll be back", and that they'd see me at the beginning of 2nd service. But then, I began giving them the same choice, "Would you like to go to Sunday school, or an early lunch?" *What?* Please don't judge! I liked having my children around!

Well, you can guess what they chose most of the time. They wanted to be with their mother AND they probably were hungry by then too!

It had only been a few weeks since I'd started this new "ritual" and as I dropped the children off at the door back at the church after our meal, I preceded on to park the car. On this day, however, when I reached over to unbuckle my seat belt, I was suddenly overcome with a voice that spoke *in* my head and *to* my heart . . . . "Do you love food more than Me?"

"What?" pretending I hadn't understood the question. "Do you love food more than Me?" the voice was just as pronounced in It's words as the first time.

"Well, Lord . . . ." Knowing it wasn't me putting myself on the spot . . . "Um . . . No. Why, No, Lord! I don't love food more than You." I knew exactly why He was asking. Then He began showing me how I'd demonstrated the opposite of my own answer. I had even been a bad example for my children! And I knew none of the excuses I'd try to use would do anything for my defense.

After I apologized profusely, He gave me a solution to my hunger problem, and I couldn't wait till the next Sunday to try it out.

Each day of the "work week" clicked off one by one. We'd had a good time as a family on Saturday night going out for a movie together. On Sunday morning, Mike headed off to the Bow Club to help set up targets for a tournament while the children and I got ready for church. I was looking forward to putting into practice what the Lord had taught me the Sunday before, and the first step to my obedience, was to "be prepared".

After getting dressed, I went to the kitchen while the children ate their "Eggos" and dug into the bottom drawer of the refrigerator. Pulling out an orange, I peeled and separated it to eatable pieces. Throwing them in a Ziploc baggie, I grabbed a 'bottled water' to go.

At the end of 1st service at church, my children waved to me from across the sanctuary, as they stood with their teacher, and I walked into my old classroom. When I found a seat between a couple of people that were eating donuts, I pulled out my juicy slices of orange. It was only moments before our new appointed teacher stood in front of the class to "get started".

"Wow. This is nice", I thought to myself, as the teacher began his lesson on the subject of "Priorities".

In the large nearly full classroom, folks continued to enjoy their sweets and coffee. Fully into the story, our speaker began to take comments from the members of his class. "Share with me your opinions on this story of these two women" he invited. Several people took the time to add a bit of how the story spoke to them. Two of the stories shared on that occasion, have stayed with me to this day:

The first was a quiet woman, probably in her late thirties. She raised her hand hesitantly and when called on, said "It's good to have friends over and to cook for and make over them, but the most important thing, is Jesus." I thought that it was very eloquently stated, but almost immediately after the obviously humble woman got the last word out of her mouth, one of the "well known" women in the church loudly spoke up, grinning and looking at her friends beside her . . . . "Well, there's a lot to do when people come over! If *we* don't do it, how's it gonna get done?" Then she smugly grinned again at the women on either side of her.

"Wow." I was kind of taken aback by her bold, almost rebellious statement. I don't remember what anyone *else's* face looked like, but I know *my* eyebrows must have been raised. Our instructor, not long after that ended his lesson with, "Martha may have been a hard worker and kept herself busy doing helpful activities, but it was Mary who had sought after the most important thing; and that was JESUS." Then our mentor left us with a question to ponder: "Are you a Mary or a Martha?"

Chapter Twenty-four

I Know Lord; You 'Got This'

And not only so, but we glory in tribulations, also: knowing that tribulation worketh patience; And patience, experience; and experience, hope: And hope maketh not ashamed; because the love of God is shed abroad in our hearts by the Holy Ghost which is given unto us. Romans 5:3-5

It was November, and 3 months since I'd been given the "Stocking Position" at Walmart. My tuition payments for the children's school along with other bills I was to pay, were becoming more difficult to make with each month that passed. I found myself "squeezing" by as I made the $7.50 and hour on my job. I made sure I kept this financial difficulty to myself. There were people out there, however, that *were* aware of my recent "job search"; and one day . . . Yes, one Glorious Day . . . . The Heaven's were opened unto me.

It was a chilly yet sunny morning, when while taking the children to Good Shepherd School, I decided to walk into the classroom with them. After telling a couple of the students "hello", one of Joshua and Kathy's teachers caught me heading back towards the door to leave. "I heard you were looking for a job", the pleasant voice said. I turned back to her and spoke, "Yes. I've been putting some applications in here and there." My children's teacher, who knew the owners of the school very well, continued. "They may have an opening coming up soon in the "Newborn through 2 year olds"; you think that you might be interested?" "What? Really? Well . . ." I stammered a bit, wondering how to ask her nicely, just how much the position paid. Before I could get the words out, she added, "Yes, and if you *WORK* for Good Shepherd School, your children get FREE TUITION!" Well, you could have knocked me down with a toothpick! "Are you serious?" I asked, ending with my mouth left hung opened. "Oh, yes, quite serious. I have 2 children in the school myself. And on top of the *free tuition*, you get a moderate hourly wage also." she added. I didn't hesitate then at all! "Who should I see to let them know that I'm interested? Where do I apply?" I spouted. She smiled and told me that she would let Mr. Kozel know that I would like to be considered for the position. I was on pins and needles for days; waiting, wondering and thinking about the load it would take off of me financially. "Me? Work as a teacher in a Christian School?" I would have never thought it possible.

About a week later, I was called in for an interview. The folks there were very professional and kind. They allowed me to meet the other teacher I would be working with and also some of the children, that is, IF I was to be given the job.

It was a couple of long weeks before I knew for sure that I had the job. I mean they were "looooong weeks". I wasn't very patient either! "Oh, Lord! When are they going to call me? *ARE* they going to call me? I know, You 'got this' LORD; I know, You 'got this.'"

After my 'patience' lesson was over, the school *did* give me that call. And when the day came that I was able to turn my little "stockers smock" back into Walmart, I was "blown away" at all the LORD had done for the children and for me.

We hold that man is never so near grace

as when he begins to feel

he can do nothing at all.

C.H. Spurgeon

Chapter Twenty-five

Be Careful Who You Pray For

Till we all come in the unity of the faith, and of the knowledge of the Son of God, unto a perfect man, unto the measure of the stature of the fullness of Christ: Ephesians 4:13

It was year 2000, and everyone had made it through what they thought would be "Black outs" and "all kinds of glitches" in technology. Joshua, Kathy and I had lots of time on our hands now that I was working the same hours that they were in school. Mike was busy at the Bow Club a lot. He loved the competitiveness of the "tournaments" and hunting season "Trophy Bucks".

Back at the First Church of the Nazarene, everything was going wonderfully. All the glitches had been worked out of the double services and Sunday school. My children were enjoying classes with other children their age; some would even come to spend the night with us on weekends. I was "loving" being part of the choir and driving the Church Van on Wednesday nights. Sometimes, the church would have Professional singers come in like *Spiritbound*, *The Talley Trio*, and *Larnelle Harris*. We were able to help out in the booths during breaks and after the concerts, in the selling of their CDs and such. Joshua, Kathy and I were involved in many "fund raisers and celebrations" We even worked together in the cotton candy and snow cone booths!

While at Choir Practice one Wednesday night, we had all taken our regular seats: Sopranos were at one end, facing the Altos at the other end; Tenors and Bass were lined on the longest wall. I noticed from across the room, in the Alto section, one of the mothers of my daughter's friend.

Her face was puffy and a little red. She looked like she had been crying. During prayer requests that night, she raised her hand and asked for us to remember her husband, Dennis, who was also a member of the choir. I looked to Dennis' regular seat, and sure enough, he was not there.

I overheard some folks talking after practice saying that Dennis was visiting another church, and Karen, his wife, did not want to leave our church to go there. They said that the situation was causing marital problems. I began to pray for them as a couple and for their children, who I knew well.

The next Wednesday night, I saw Dennis' chair empty again. And again, I saw Karen's troubled state. I continued to pray.

A couple of weeks later, I received a phone call. "Hello?" I paused to hear a response. "Hi LuAnn? This is Karen; you know, from choir." "Oh, yes, Karen. How are you doing?" I tried to sound upbeat and not like I knew all of her business. She went on: "I'm doing well. Actually, I was calling to invite you to a Bible Study. It's on Tuesday night, here at my house. You think you may want to come?" She waited for my answer. "Well, sure, Karen, I believe I can come on that night. What time?" I could not believe that I had just said "Yes." to an invitation to a Bible Study. I NEVER say "yes" to anything like "Tupperware Parties, Jewelry Parties, Handbag Parties," etc. I was a person with a rigid schedule, for heaven's sake. After Karen gave me the time that this "Bible Study" was supposed to start, I marked it on my calendar.

Hanging up the phone from talking with her, I still did not understand how "Yes" got out of my mouth before my brain kicked in to "turn her down". "Did I say "Yes" because I had been feeling bad for her and praying, or did I day "yes" because inside, I really wanted to go learn more about God's Word? Well, for whatever reason, I am going to "show up"."

And "show up" I did. On the following Tuesday night, I came to Karen's home with Bible and notebook in hand. While there, I was introduced to a salt and pepper haired man they called "Pastor Gus". There were only 4 of us there, along with Pastor Gus; One lady from our church, and another from Dennis' workplace plus Karen and me. After introductions, we all proceeded to the dining room and took a seat at Karen's oval shaped table. We joined in for a quick prayer, and the "study" we'd all come for, began.

While Pastor Gus spoke, his eyes sparkled softly as he shared with boldness, scripture from God's Word. He gave us, that night, some details about the Mosaic Tabernacle and how it relates to "growing in Christ". My eyes widened several times, and I had him go over a couple of points twice, even more amazed the second time than the first. I had heard lots of sermons preached and taught many times during my life, but something seemed different on that night. I saw how being a Christian was not just about asking JESUS into your heart, and trying to live a Godly life, but to include the furthering of one's Spiritual Growth. And I was seeing with my own eyes for the first time in my Bible! (Ephesians 4:11-16)

The next Tuesday, I attended this Bible Study again, and the next and the next! I was so excited about having "opened", now, these deep crevasses of God's Word that I'd never been aware of before.

I continued to go to my home church as before, but with each week that passed, I grew more and more hungry for God's Word. "If the Bible Studies are this intense at Karen's when Pastor Gus is teaching us, I wonder how their church services are." I thought. So, one week, I asked the head of the Van Ministries at the Nazarene Church if they would find someone to take my route for the upcoming Wednesday night. After all bases were covered, I was free to visit this little church in the nearby town of Dayton.

Chapter Twenty-six

Just Like I Feel Inside

Love the LORD your God with all your heart and with all your soul and with all your strength. Deuteronomy 6:5

It was nearing 6 pm, and I slipped on my little white dress shoes. I really wanted to be in Dayton by 6:30 pm. "Karen told me that the folks at this Christ Gospel Church begin prayer at that time." I was thinking as I grabbed my Bible and notebook. I wanted to take in all I could about this church tonight, after all, I'd only asked for one night off from my usual duties as Van Driver.

The Tuesday night Bible Studies had ministered to my heart so, that my anticipation grew with each mile I drove on the way.

"Okay, she said, down Highway 42, passed Walmart, yes. Walmart was there on the right. Then right onto Eberly Road; Left onto Main Street. Mmm. Okay. Got it." As I drove the directions Karen had given me, I noticed the rolling green hills of farmland becoming more abundant. Cows grazed casually in the roadside fields. "Over the little bridge and right . . . here, at the old Texaco Station." I continued reading the directions from a slip of paper in my hand. There were quant little homes and businesses lined along the roads. Family members strolled hand in hand down the stretch of sidewalk. "Okay. I should be getting close. Ah! There it is." After halting for a couple of sets of 4-way stop signs, I spotted the small older looking church on the left. Cars were parked along the side of the streets surrounding the building across from the Dayton Learning Center, so I followed suit, and parked. Looking myself over once more, I exited the car while grabbing my Bible and notebook.

Taking a stroll up the sidewalk, as if I was a local resident, I took in the sweet fragrance of Bluebell flowers blooming.

As I neared the large shiny pine green door of the church, I heard the faint sound of soothing music coming from the windows and entrance. Even more driven than before, I pressed down on the aged brass-looking door latch and pushed the door open.

Gentle melodies filled the carpeted, dimmed sanctuary. My eyes fell on the many individuals, knelt by the Alter and at their seats in prayer. The sounds I heard were strangely familiar, and I recognized them from my youth. The beautiful voices blended in harmony as they spoke in melodious tongues to their LORD and King.

Moving slowly and quietly, not to interrupt their praying, I eased into the seat saved for me at the far side of the room. Placing the books on the padded red chair, I went to my knees and joined them in prayer.

Time passed quickly, and I hadn't even noticed the band and worship team had made their way to the platform. The service transcended smoothly from recorded tranquil music into the onstage vocals and instruments. The lights were raised to a still conservative level as people here and there rose from the floor to their feet. Voices slowly began to join their leaders in song until all were standing. In worshipful praise, some raised their hands as they tilted their tear covered faces to the heavens. Again, I felt such freedom, as I lifted my own voice, heart and hands to JESUS with them. One song after another was offered as in "wonder", I stood at my place. "These people, they worship Him like no other I've seen" I thought. "They don't act afraid or intimidated, or ashamed to express their love and gratitude for Him." I had not witnessed anything like it before. Nothing had even come close.

After a few songs, that had graduated from slow and moderate, to fast, bouncy and joyful, the music ended. The congregation was told that they could find their seats. I figured it was time for the sermon, and it was, but just before we went to the WORD, Pastor Gus had us to all stand up and hold our Bibles high. One of the men prayed over The Word and we sat down again. The message was so awesome that night. While the Pastor was preaching, I looked around, and almost EVERY person in the church was taking notes! I had brought my own notebook, but had no idea that these folks made a habit of taking notes too during service. Every once in a while I would hear one or two of the men say, "Amen!" or "Hallelujah!", and sometimes, the whole congregation would get so excited about the Word being preached that they would jump or shout. I even saw someone run back and forth across the front in his excitement!

During closing prayer that night, all but one of my questions had been answered. After service, lots of folks shook my hand nicely. When I looked into each of these persons' eyes, I could see the sincerity and love they offered to their fellow sister in Christ. I noticed the preacher's wife smiling my way, and I met her at the exit door. I requested an answer for the question that had been burning in my mind . . . "What is that star thing with a cross in it "stand for"?" "Oh, yes . . . that is the Star Of David. (It was a Jewish symbol, like what is on Israel's flag) It has a cross in it because Jesus is the Messiah." She had answered me so gently; I'd almost wished I'd had another question for her. But I thanked her for allowing me to join them for service. She smiled again and thanked me for coming.

As I returned home, I could not stop thinking about all I had observed. "These people . . . they express their love for God so well; it's in a way that's . . . *just like I feel inside!* I must find out more about them. I must return."

Chapter Twenty-seven

Now We Know

Train up a child in the way he should go: and when he is old, he will not depart from it. Proverbs 22:6

After many more weeks of Tuesday night Bible Studies and several visits to their church, when responsibilities would allow, I became more and more convinced that Christ Gospel Church was where the LORD wanted me to be. I was Spiritually Hungry and the things I was learning about myself and about Christ were helping me. Each message Pastor Gus preached, spoke to my heart in a way that made me want to do more, to be more, to love others more, in Christ. And with each time I attended CGC, the bolder I became about speaking Jesus' Name in everyday conversations, as I thanked Him for all He'd done for me in my life.

You're probably asking by now, "What about your children? Where were they in all this?" Well, I have an answer for you!

Major changes such as these are rough for all of us, and especially for children. I attended periodically, and for a few weeks, the Christ Gospel Church without Joshua and Kathy, because I wanted to "check it out" before moving them from the First Church of the Nazarene. I had no idea, though, what had been going on in those sweet little young minds during that period, until, the very first Sunday I shared this little "Goldmine of God's Word" with them.

It was the very first Sunday we were going to attend Christ Gospel Church as a family. Oh, except for Mike. He went to the Bow Club. Joshua and Kathy had heard several descriptions of the church and its people from me, but more than that, they had never heard me talk this much about Jesus, so openly.

As we took our places in the somewhat small, aged sanctuary, the Worship Team and its band began to lead us in a song. While singing to the Lord, I smiled at each of my children standing beside me. They knew this song we were singing. It had been on one of the children's tapes I had bought for them years ago. The people at this Christ Gospel Church were just as exuberant about JESUS that day, as they had been the other times I had visited alone. While people went to the Alter to pray, Kathy began to cry at her seat. Her friend Kayla had been sitting beside her and she had joined Kathy in praying; she was crying also! Joshua seemed to enjoy being there, and was very respectful and he reverenced the atmosphere surrounding him.

After we were dismissed, I looked at my watch in disbelief! It was already 1 pm and it only felt like 11:30 or 12! The Word, Worship, and the whole atmosphere had been so incredible, we had not even noticed the time till then.

Walking across the street to where we had parked, Joshua and Kathy were buzzing. "Mom! Mom! Now we know what you were talking about!! They were laughing and Kathy was practically skipping along the road. "Mom, we have something to tell you . . ." I paused, smiling and said, "Yes? What? What?" I waited for their response and they kept looking at each other and laughing. "Mom, we were really getting sick of being around you because you were just so happy . . . and you kept talking about JESUS." I looked at them both, a little surprised at their confession, as they continued. "Mom, now we know. Now we know WHY you were so happy and WHY you kept talking about HIM. We understand your excitement! We're so glad you brought us here." And that was that! After I informed the head of the "Van Ministry" at the Nazarene Church that I could only drive for them for two more weeks, the children and I began attending Christ Gospel Church of Dayton on a regular basis.

Chapter Twenty-eight

Leading & Feeding

That ye put off concerning the former conversation the old man, which is corrupt according to the deceitful lusts; And be renewed in the spirit of your mind; And that ye put on the new man, which after God is created in righteousness and true holiness.
Ephesians 4:22-24

Over the next few weeks and months, the children and I learned more of how to "grow in Christ". They taught us about the "Old Man" which is our "Self", and what it wants, verses, the "New Man" inside of us, which is the Lord Jesus Christ! And when we make everyday choices, we're either being "led by" one of those two, or "feeding" one or the other. (i.e. the Old or New Man) It all made perfect sense!

Christ Gospel Church was filled with folks who were not afraid to express their gratitude and admiration of the LORD Jesus Christ. I used to think that something was wrong with me because I wanted to talk about Him and relate my surroundings to Him. Anything and everything that happened around me, I knew it was Him desiring to teach me something. I thought it was a common thing around Christian people, but I soon found myself believing that I was strange. Even back when I was in choir, during practice, Pastor Joe had made it a habit of asking for "Praises" along with "Prayer Requests". Well, there's always something to give the LORD praise over, right? One night, while asking for any "Praise reports" he worded it like this: "Does anyone have "A Praise" tonight . . . besides LuAnn that is?" And that was before I even raised my hand! I knew he was teasing, and I took it in stride, but that incident, along with others, made me feel that maybe I should begin "backing off" or "backing up" a little. "Perhaps I should not talk about or think about the LORD *so* much", I thought. But just as I began to think that, He opened the door to a wonderful Spiritual Family at Christ Gospel Church. They walked and talked and thought like I did. I found I did NOT need to "be quiet" about the One I loved.

And please, as you read this, do not believe I think more highly of myself than I ought to. Actually, it's to the contrary that makes me want to shout His praises from the rooftops! You see, sometimes one must get to the bottom before "he" or "she" finally "looks up"! And that's where I have come from; the bottom.

If you, as the reader, interpreted the first 10 or 15 chapters, you know where the LORD rescued *me* from. He rescued me from ME.

In *Luke 7:40-48*, God's Word tells us that the one who has had the greatest debt and is released of it is usually the most grateful; whether it is a debt of money or sin, the same seems to apply. So, you see, it is nothing I have done, and it is EVERYTHING that HE has done.

When the children and I first made the move to Christ Gospel Church, my husband questioned our decision. "Why you want to go to that church? It's an old looking building, it's small and doesn't even have as many members as the Nazarene Church?" he asked. And even though Mike had not been going to church with us, I wanted to help him understand. I had not given up hope that he would come, eventually with us.

The LORD gave me just the right analogy that would help him understand. "Well, honey, if you were a member of a Big and well known Bow club with lots of members . . . ." (And he was) " . . . and you had a great time there, but you had the desire to learn more about hunting with a "bow" . . . (he reeeeally related there) " . . . . and there was a smaller bow club down the road that had a couple of men there that were willing to teach you the expertise of bow hunting . . . ." Mike was still listening intently as I went on. " . . . then, would you be willing to move to THAT small bow club to learn, or would you stay at the other one just to say you belonged to a large prestigious one?"

He was stumped. I don't remember that he ever gave me his answer to that question, but I felt satisfied that I had explained it well.

At this point, you may, again, be wondering about the children? After all, wasn't my obligation, my promise to the LORD, to raise them to "Know Him" and "His Love"? How did I know that this was to be their church?

Why yes, it was my obligation and my promise. And that's why I'm excited to share with you this: Only a few weeks after we began to attend "Christ Gospel", Joshua told me that he had been offered marijuana several times from his friends before coming to that church. He had made up his mind THAT very week prior to coming to CGC, that he was going to "smoke pot" with his friends. But after the first Sunday at our new church, he said, "Mom, I could not do it then! It's like I found what I needed and it was not "pot"." I was amazed at the LORD's timing.

Kathy shared with me, also, only a short time after we'd moved: "Mom, before, when songs were sung, or while we prayed at our old church, I had to fight back what I was feeling inside. If I wanted to go to the Alter or if I cried at my seat, everyone would look at me strange, or ask me, "Aw. Are you okay?" But now, I don't have to fight it when I feel convicted or joyful. I can cry and pray, even go to the Alter, and there are others there doing the same thing. It's not looked at as *strange*! I can be myself, Mom!"

Our sweet Kathy was baptized for the first time, at CGC about a month after we came there. She, many times had refused that opportunity at the church before. After coming to CGC, Joshua and I rededicated our lives to Christ, and chose to be "rebaptized". Kathy used her gift of painting, to capture her brother's baptism on canvas.

The LORD was doing wonders in our family and with us, as individuals. He has a plan, a path for all of His Children's lives. Two questions are: Do we want it? Are we willing to follow it?

There is not a person, a group, a church, a gift or a miracle that should be worshipped. It is the LORD Jesus Christ that deserves all our praise!

The Baptist Church I was brought up in taught my parents and us kids so much "Word". When I began attending the Nazarene Church, they taught my family about a personal relationship with Jesus Christ. Now, at this Christ Gospel Church, which is considered to be somewhat

"Pentecostal", we were learning Spiritual Growth. I am amazed and so grateful for each "Stepping Stone" the LORD gives us in our walk with Him.

After only a couple of weeks there, at our new church, I could tell, already, that my heart was becoming more forgiving, caring and quite aware of how I could be more like Jesus each day. The children were continually excited about learning and growing too. I could see big changes in their confidence, obedience and outlook on their futures as they served God. It is so true, that when Christ is the Head of your home, everything falls in place and you are unified through having that Godhead leadership to correctly make everyday decisions and choices. When one falls, the others are there to help pick them back up. It seems it would be the ultimate way to live—living for Jesus, but when one does not choose God, sometimes those who do, actually begin to ruffle the other's feathers without even being aware their choice has done so. Some people just hate change. But what if it's change for the better?

Chapter Twenty-nine

He Is Faithful

Rejoice greatly, O daughter of Zion; shout, O daughter of Jerusalem: behold, thy King cometh unto thee: he is just, and having salvation; lowly, and riding upon an ass, and upon a colt the foal of an ass. Zechariah 9:9

My husband had been "tolerant" of my "Christianity" thus far; from 1994 to the present. Mike even had answers for his buddies when they had discussed my tithing to the church before. Mike jokingly shared with me what he'd said, "Yea, she doesn't buy much for herself; she just gives money to the church, and me? Well, I buy all this stuff." as he points to his many tree stands, rifles, bows, motorcycle, 4-wheeler, and truck. Mike worked hard. He took very good care of what he purchased for himself, and I admired him greatly for it.

I had begun to notice that Mike was spending a lot more time at the "Bow Club", however and less time at home. He'd been buying new clothes and dressing a little differently. He'd even lost some weight. One day, Mike told me that because of the increase in gas prices, he was going to start looking for a small used car to travel the 30 minutes to work and back each day. That sounded good to me. We had always made it a point to live on a budget. It was a pretty lenient one, however, and the allotment for items was greater than what we would spend each month.

Mike took a trip to his Mom's in Tennessee one weekend. On one of his calls home, he told me that he was at the "Bill Gatton Dealership" and had found a vehicle. He went on to tell me that the one he'd picked out was a New Oldsmobile Alero; Bright Red, with sunroof, leather interior—the works. He asked what I thought about him buying it. He sounded really happy and I did not want to deny him this pleasure, but I had to be truthful. "I really don't think we can afford a brand new car, Mike." He didn't seem to be upset that I'd made that statement, but he did try to reason the opposite with me. At the end of the conversation, I told him, "Mike, you can do whatever you feel is right."

Before he came home on Sunday, he phoned to say that he had purchased the new car.

When he returned home in his original vehicle, he asked if I would go back with him the next weekend and help him get the car home; he drove one and I, the other. We went the following weekend.

When we returned from our trip to Tennessee, Mike informed me that he was separating our incomes and dividing up the bills. I had been in charge of paying bills for many years, at his request. Now, with the incomes and bills separated, it partly was a relief to me, but since I knew his "reasons" and "motives" behind that decision, it was a very "hurtful" time. I'd always wanted him to be happy. His happiness, along with the "children's" was always at the forefront of my heart and mind. I had labeled myself a "Pleaser" long before this happened.

I believe that my "giving" to the church had become as "issue" with him. And when I did not give the answer he wanted to hear about the purchase of the new car, I'd provoked him to swing the hammer that was eventually destined to fall.

Although Mike had written in some hefty bills on my side of the line drawn on the paper he'd handed me, I took this assignment in stride. And THAT means, I did not complain or cry to him, but I did shed a few tears later while talking to the LORD, for He knows all things, and cares for us oh so very much. After several days of anxiety from my "guts" churning because of my husband's anger and his holding back of his affection from me, there eventually came a peace . . . a rest. I had prayed and cried until I was dry, then I knew everything would be alright.

I continued to give to the church by faith, and went back to the old reliable: "The Classifieds". There, in black and white, I spotted a request for a part-time Hairdresser at a Healthcare Facility! Wow! I had looked for a job like that when I first came to Harrisonburg! Now, if I could apply and "get on" there, it would serve as a little "extra" money, to add to the income at my regular job!

When I visited the facility, it was simply beautiful. The "shop" was near the entrance to the place, and just as before, I was allowed to set my own days and hours.

It was quite sometime before Mike even knew I had a second job, because he was gone a lot. The "fun" thing about working there, was when I would get home, and Mike was not, I would take the children out to the local "diner" and have quality time with them talking and laughing. Joshua, to this day says that he "loved" those Pano's fried oysters.

I seemed to have more money than I ever did! And although the "split" of money and bills looked "hopeless" on my end, it was like the LORD was "stretching" each dollar, as I continued to tithe on the income.

Three months had passed and our seventh Christmas in Virginia was upon us. Usually, as this time of year drew close, we would limit our purchases and agree to spend a moderate amount on each child. We always made it a point to give Kathy, Joshua and Kayla gifts that cost the same. But this year, since incomes were our own, I took the liberty to spend what I wanted to on the children and Mike. Mike took care of Kayla's present and I bought Joshua and Kathy's. When Joshua came back from visiting his Dad during the holidays, he arrived home to an awesome dark grey and wood grained desk. It took up almost 2 walls of his bedroom. He was into studying, computers and gaming, and it was the perfect gift for him. And upon Kathy's return, I surprised her with a rose and white "daybed" AND a video camera!

Mike and I had spent a little time together while the children were away at their dad's. He saw that I was doing well with my "end" of the bills and seemed genuinely happy that Joshua and Kathy received the gifts they had. It was like he respected me. Yes, that's what I saw in his eyes: *Respect*.

The Lord had worked everything out so well. I won't lie to you; it was scary at first, as I followed my desire to trust Him with the situation I was in. But just as He promises to take care of us, He did. Oh! I never told you the name of the Healthcare Facility the Lord had given me employment in! It was:

"King's Daughters"

God, who foresaw your tribulation,

has specially armed you to go through it,

not without pain but without stain.

C.S. Lewis

Chapter Thirty

Choose This Day
Whom You Will Serve

Choose this day whom you will serve; as for me and my house, we will serve the LORD. Joshua 24:15 b, d

It was March of 2002. Mike had announced he was going to "Bike Week" in Daytona, Florida with some buddies. I knew he had wanted to go, but years ago, we'd gone together. He hadn't asked me to go this time. I guess I should have expected it. The last time he went to a NASCAR Race in Bristol, Tennessee, he'd not asked me to go either. He said he was meeting his brother and his brother's fiancée there. We'd kind of been leading separate lives lately, except for some meals and a bed. He spent a lot of time at the bow club, and had hopes of being elected their next President. The children and I continued to attend church and some activities there, when they did not interfere with our time with Mike.

Since my husband had made plans to go to Daytona with friends, I let him know that the children and I would take a couple of days and visit my parents in North Carolina while he was gone. He didn't say much about it. He hadn't been talking much to me lately. It seemed the more I wanted to "be good" or "do what was right", the more he despised me. He'd made comments to me over the past few months like, "You're just trying to be an angel" and "you used to love me more than God, but now you love God more than me." I wanted to make him happy . . . I was used to doing things to make him smile and laugh. He hadn't been smiling or laughing too much around me lately. I felt like a disappointment to him every time I looked into his eyes. But what can one do? Should I smoke, drink and cuss to be that "girl he'd married long ago?" I didn't want to be her.

It seemed the more I secretly prayed for the LORD to help my husband, the more I saw him drink. He hadn't done that but occasionally before, but lately, it was every night.

One evening just a few days shy of his planned trip, Kathy was with friends and Joshua at the neighbors. Mike had driven up the driveway. As he came into the house, he wore the look again; the face that contained the empty eyes, from where I used to see such love. A furrowed brow had taken the spotlight from what used to be smile lines beside his lashes. He pulled out a fifth of George Dickel from a brown bag and helped himself to a drink.

When he spoke, it was to tell me that he wanted to sit with me a few minutes. I threw a load of laundry into the dryer, and then took a seat next to him on the couch.

After he downed the rest of his drink, he began to discuss what was on his mind. "I can't live like this anymore, LuAnn. You've changed." I felt a "stab" in my gut as his words registered. "You've been changing ever since we came to Virginia." At that point I didn't know whether to "thank him for the compliment" or "explain why". I chose the latter and tried to rationalize with him, "But I'm a better wife, a better mother and a better person all around, because I have Jesus in my heart. I want to be "good" and "kind", "loving" and "forgiving". But he told me that I was okay the way I used to be. He missed the "old me." He then created his own analogy to help me understand: "If I started smoking pot, and bringing it home, and smoking it here without you and I discussing it first would that be fair to you?"

I could not believe he was using this example to try and prove a point. "But Mike, smoking pot is illegal! And how does it compare to wanting to change for the better?" He was so determined to let me know how much my "change" had "messed" this marriage up, that I guess he was grasping at any straw he could.

"Well, we're going to get to the bottom of this when I get home, LuAnn. You are going to go back to the way you used to be, or I'll just put this house up for sale and we'll go our separate ways . . . no, better yet, I'll find out how much the house is worth and I'll buy you out, how about that?" I sat, with my head down, clicking my thumbnails against each other nervously. "Okay." I answered in a quiet voice. The hurt was too much to bear. "How could I be making the one I love so miserable?" I thought to myself. I could hold back the tears no longer. "Well, I guess it's a mutual split then." He hammered again. I lowered my eyes and moved my head side to side signing "no". I didn't want a divorce. He continued in a frustrated loud voice, "I see no other way, LuAnn, unless I can persuade you to change. Are you going to go back to the way you used to be?" I told him, "no." again, hesitantly. "Well, that's it then, we'll split with 'irreconcilable differences'."

After he left me sitting there, I was surprisingly calm. It's like I heard some kind of beautiful music in my ears that soothed my spirit. I had not expected this to happen on this day, but now that it was done, I was not going to fret. I didn't want a divorce, but I didn't want to continue to cause such anguish to my husband either. I still had hoped that Mike would perhaps miraculously realize that I loved him; that Jesus loved him and that Jesus died for him too.

Chapter Thirty-one

The Blessings of Bagels & 'Buddies'

My beloved spake, and said unto me,
Rise up, my love, my fair one, and come away.
For, lo, the winter is past, the rain is over and
gone; Song of Solomon 2:10-11

My husband's vacation was to take him to Bike Week in Daytona Beach, Florida, and the children and I planned a few days visiting family in North Carolina. Joshua and Kathy did not know yet, that Mike had asked me for a divorce. I wanted to wait a couple of days, in hopes that he might change his mind. The children were at Harrisonburg High School, taking their last class in Drivers Education. It was offered to anyone of "age" "homeschooling" or "private schooling" in the area.

I hadn't had much of an appetite since my encounter with Mike, the day before, but I had about a half hour before the children were to get out of their class. Pulling into the lot of Mr. J's Bagels near the school, I decided I'd try to eat. Slipping into a secluded booth, I took a bite of my bagel and sipped my drink. I was reading from a compact Bible I carried around, when I heard a man speak from the counter area that was out of my view. As I listened to the confident, steady voice, he finished placing his order. The cashier's tone and choice of words gave an impression of "flirting" as she spoke with the gentleman. I knew she was a very pretty girl, because I'd just ordered myself. Continuing to listen to the "heard and not seen" conversation, it surprised me that the man's voice did not waver as he was polite. He had not returned her inviting manner and although I'd only heard this one conversation, I was impressed by the sound of his professional response and composure.

I had just gone back to my bagel and soda when I heard footsteps drawing closer. As he passed my booth I looked up and noticed that the footsteps had come from a policeman. He nodded his head and smiled as if to say, "Hello". I smiled back and then looked down as I continued to read. I had picked a particular set of scriptures to study that was on my recent and tender subject. As the policeman walked back for, what I assume, was his order, he, again, returned to the dining area. This time, on the way back, he paused, and stood right by my table. "It sure is great to see someone still reading *that* book", he said. He continued on and took his seat on the other side of mine. The booths at the restaurant were very tall, and when sitting in them, you cannot see over the tops. In shock that he'd spoke, I looked at my Bible and responded, "Well, the Lord's done so much for me. I want to learn more about Him and how to serve Him." I felt my cheeks redden as I had stood to speak these testifying words, so that he could hear over the tall wood separating us. I'd sat back down quickly and almost found the place I'd stopped reading from, when the uniformed man stood up himself, and said, "He's done an awful lot for me too." I just nodded nicely in agreement. I felt so blessed to find there *was* a man out there who loved the Lord. It had shown me that there were people (not just at *my* church) that felt the same as I did. I wasn't crazy for loving the Lord after all.

A couple of minutes went by and I, by this time, was back in the Word. Just when I was beginning to get the "gist" of the passage, the "Man in blue" approached the booth I was in and laid a business card down on the other side of my things. "If you ever need anything, or anyone to pray with you, please give me a call", he said kindly, stepping back to his booth, disappearing once again.

I remember thinking, "What a Christ-like thing to do." I continued to read, but then glanced over at his card. On it, along with all the information and phone numbers, was his picture. I had never seen this gentleman before. I looked at his name out of curiosity. What I read took me completely by surprise. I actually thought I was mistaken and was misreading his name. It read: William (Buddy) W. Farris Jr., Chief of Police, Dayton Police Dept.

"This couldn't be the same man that died on the road after being hit by a vehicle, then pronounced dead and taken to the morgue and started breathing again. There's no way", I said to myself.

A couple of years ago I had picked up a free tape at the Daystar Bookstore in town. It was a recording of "The Buddy Farris testimony"; On it, he had shared how the Lord brought him back to life, and other wonderful things He had done for him.

I just couldn't sit any longer. I stood, one last time, and asked, "You're um . . . not the one . . . uh. (I didn't want to sound foolish, just incase I was wrong) . . . that almost . . . I mean DID . . . die and come back to life . . . uh . . . are you?" He dropped his head in humility and said, "Yes ma'am that was me." I know my eyes were the size of half dollars at that moment. I grinned and responded, "Well, I'd say, you're right! The Lord *HAS* done a lot for you." We both laughed as he responded, "Yes ma'am" one more time. I sat down and was amazed at what the LORD had shown me this very morning; *that He is still in control, even when there are storms going on all around me . . . He's there. I only need to keep my eyes focused on Him.*

I finished my bagel and ordered the children something 'to go' for when we traveled. I couldn't help but want to thank Mr. Farris. He probably had no idea how much he had encouraged me by his words and testimony. He had definitely been used by God this day.

I wrote a quick thank you note to him to let him know that in his obedience to the Lord's prompting to speak to me, I had been blessed. I shared with him, that, just a couple of days earlier I had been given an ultimatum by my husband concerning my Christianity. On the piece of paper, I thanked him for showing me that *he* was one that had chosen God.

Before delivering this note, however, I asked the Lord to please have Mr. Farris leave the restaurant before I did, if I wasn't supposed to give it to him. I waited in line, ordered the children's food and gathered my things. When their food was ready, Mr. Farris was still sitting there. I placed it on his table and said, "thank you."

When I picked up Joshua and Kathy, they knew nothing of Mike's request for a divorce. Now that they were out of school and we were on our way to North Carolina, it was time to tell them.

After we'd been on the road a while, I let them know what was going on. They sat and waited until I'd told them about Mike, and then about the words from "Buddy Farris". Expecting to hear some sadness in their voices, I was surprised when Kathy screamed out suddenly, "Mama! You must be so special to God! He raised Buddy Farris from the dead that day, just so that he could be here to tell you that! The LORD just stops the whole world in its tracks for you . . . everything comes to a "standstill" for MY Mama!" she said boldly. I started laughing and crying at the same time. "Boy, you really see the BIG Picture of things, don't you honey?" I told her. Indeed, it had turned out to be a great day, but it was only the beginning of the miraculous ones to come.

Chapter Thirty-two

I Need A Moses

Yea, though I walk through the valley of the shadow of death, I will fear no evil: for thou art with me; thy rod and thy staff they comfort me. Psalms 23:4

During the later hours of the first day the children and I were in North Carolina, I shared with my parents the burden that troubled me. My Dad advised me, "You need to call Mike right now, and ask him if he will change his mind." I made the phone call to my now estranged husband, as Dad asked, and Mike's reply was not good. He was supposed to leave for Daytona two days after I left for NC, but he informed me on the phone that he had NOT changed his mind about the divorce, but he *had* made a change in plans concerning his trip. He was now leaving a day sooner. It wasn't the answer I'd hoped for. I was determined not to ruin the next few days I would be spending with my parents, so I kept my chin up, listened to some more advice from my father and continued to socialize with my extended family members there. I avoided mentioning the depressing news again that day.

The following morning, I woke in the room I'd had as a child. Ah, what a comfort it was. Then I began to recall some of my husband's hurtful words from the day before and all I felt like doing was burying my head back into the pillow in hopes that it would all "go away". I started to cry. I asked the Lord to help me be strong. I told Him that I just could not do this alone. With my face buried into my pillow, the sounds of my brokenness were muffled. "Lord, I need a Moses to lead me through", I prayed. I knew I was weak, weary and definitely not strong enough to be the leader that it would take to make it through this tough time with my children. I felt like we were the Israelites and we'd been given our "walking papers" after Pharaoh was sick of all the plagues and death. I didn't allow my parents see me cry that morning. I was not going to show my sadness. "I didn't come here for pity. I came to spend time with my family." I assured myself. "And I'm going to do just that."

I went for a walk that morning. It was sunny, yet a mild temperature outside. I loved going for walks in NC. I suppose it's because they have less hilly terrain and I'm able to enjoy the scenery more. Well, I'll just admit it; it was still Home to me, although we had been away for 7 years.

As I walked on this bright morning, I sang some "praise songs" to the LORD. I took the "blocked out circular route" I always had; the one my dad had shown me before his knees got too bad for him to go along.

I noticed, while I was on the last part of my walk, a Robin sitting near the road, at the edge of a local resident's lush lawn. I took a couple of glances at the bird, because it looked unusually fat; it was about as big as two birds would have been! On reexamination, I concluded it had indeed, only been one. Afterwards, I continued back to the house.

After lunch on the same day, I decided another walk would be nice. I had a lot of thinking and praying to do. Again, I followed the same route and on last part of the walk, I passed by where the "fat bird" had been. I glanced to see if the Robin was still there, and it was not. I had almost begun my walk again, when something caught my eye. There, in the grass, right where the Robin had been, I saw what appeared to be a small stick of some sort. As I drew closer, I discovered that it was a long stick. It was very smooth in appearance. I picked it up just to satisfy my urge to feel its surface. As I did, I was surprised to find a crook at one end of it. Why, it was similar to a hand carved cane or walking stick. Then, it flew through my mind, "Thy rod and thy staff, they comfort me . . ." I looked around to see if someone had left it there by the road. There was no one around. The nearest house was too far for it to belong to someone there. I made another scan, attempting to reason this out. There was no explanation for this stick lying where a bird had been.

I restarted my walking; now carrying this new inspiration along with me. I had only gotten a few steps when it hit me . . . "I had asked for a

Moses this morning!" By this time, I was ready to run! Off I went to Dad and Mom's house. I couldn't wait to tell them! "They will surely believe I'm crazy." I thought. I dismissed that notion just as quickly as it had come. "I don't care if they do. If they don't believe this came from God, I can't help it. I believe . . . I MUST believe." I sighed.

I approached the house and ran to the door. Mom was the first one I saw. I shared with her excitedly, what had happened and I was so overcome with joy that I didn't even notice her reaction. We told Dad also. I don't believe he knew what to think. Suddenly, I had the strength and courage I needed. I knew what the Lord was trying to show me; He'd be with me through it, all the way.

My little nephew, Brandon came to visit at Mom and Dad's that day, and we shared the exciting story of what had happened. I snapped this picture while he was there.

Nephew Brandon with the "Moses' Rod"

That very night, I attended the church I'd belonged to as a child, with Dad and Mom. Yes! It was Andrews Memorial Baptist Church!

After the singing and announcements were over and the sermon began, Mom and I almost had to pick our jaws up off the sanctuary floor when the pastor started preaching on Moses. Out of all the people in God's Word that he could have preached about, he was led to speak about Moses. Across the wide smiles Mom and I wore on our faces, tears fell in streams; and I've never heard my Mom say, "Amen" and "Praise The Lord" as much as I did that night during the sermon.

I had no trouble falling asleep *that* night, for it felt like I was right in my Heavenly Father's arms. He made me know that I was special to Him and that He had not left me, or forgotten me.

When I returned to my home church in Virginia only a couple of days later, I shared with my Pastor and his wife what had happened. They looked at each other and smiled as if they had a secret. They let me know that they had just returned from a Pastor's Convention in Indiana. "LuAnn, you are not going to believe what Reverend Hicks taught on there", my Pastor said. I looked at them both, wide-eyed and curious. They confessed, "It was on Moses and the rod".

I will never forget what The Lord did for me that week. No matter how small and insignificant we may be in the world, He knows us, and He cares for us; each and every one.

Chapter Thirty-three

Parting Ways & Finding Home

He that dwelleth in the secret place of the most High shall abide under the shadow of the Almighty. Psalm 91:1

The next few weeks were tough ones, I must admit. Living under a roof with someone who used to love you, and now doesn't, presents a lot of uncomfortableness and hurt for all parties involved.

Mike had made it clear that there was no longer a "perhaps" or "maybe" about going our separate ways, so I began to look for a home for the children and me. I didn't want to pay rent for a while and then end up moving again; and as easy as it would have been to pick up everything and move back to North Carolina, I knew that my children and I were learning so much in God's Word, that it would be a mistake.

I had purposefully driven the streets of decent neighborhoods, and searched online for houses for sale. I did not want to stay in our "Bridle Court" home any longer than necessary.

I had no Real-estate agent particularly assigned to me. I didn't even think it mattered. I would just see a house, call the number posted and they'd "show up" to open it for me. I had been "hitting the streets" for about a week or two by myself.

Kathy wanted to go "house hunting" with me on one of the days I was off, so away we went. I don't recall why we decided to go down the street named "Rockingham", but it does have a church on the corner of it. I'd grown up on a street with a church across the way, so it seemed kind of familiar. As we eased slowly down this shaded "back road", we spotted a little white house on the right, sitting on a small incline of a hill. There were two huge trees in the front yard and a rolling thick blacktopped driveway leading the way to the door.

I had looked at the outside of so many houses, and called for information about some, but not until my daughter was with me that day, had I felt this good about one. Kathy and I both agreed that there was something about this house that stood out to us. Out front there was a sign stuck in the yard and a number for a Lori Clouse. We jetted to the nearest payphone and called her. Lori told us she would meet us at that location within a few moments.

As we waited for the realtor, we peeped into one of the windows and walked through the back yard. When Lori arrived and opened the doors up for us, it was the "icing on the cake"! The kitchen and one of the three bedrooms had wood paneling. The bathrooms had the same color of tiles of the home I'd grown up in! The house was laid out in the same way *that one* was too! It was like being back in North Carolina again, in my parents' home! Lori shared that if we were to purchase this property, that we would have neighbors of the older generation. Our view from the front door was that of a Rock Quarry, and the back, was that of mountains.

We told Lori that we wanted to make an offer on the house that day. The "asking price" of the property was $78,500. I had figured out a budget, according to a Christian Budgeting Class I'd taken. Cendent Mortgage had approved me for a large amount of money, but I let them know how much I'd wanted my payments to be, and they gave me these figures: I was to put down a sum of $15,000 and borrow $60,000 for a home. Okay, you do the figures! I wanted to make an offer of $75,000, but Lori told me that the "offer" had a better chance of being considered if I offered $78,500 with the stipulation that they pay the $3,500 closing cost. We chose to do it that way on that very day.

The realtor called me later and told me she'd found out that the very same offer had been made previously, and had been turned down. I prayed that if the Lord wanted us to have *this* house, the man would take the offer. I was sticking to the price I'd offered and "move on" if this was not the one for us. I prayed for the Lord's perfect Will.

We had given the owner a few days to think the offer over. It was nearing the end of the allotted time for their "pondering" when we found out that they had been out of town. Lori and I had just discussed giving them a couple of more days to think about it, when she received the news . . . . They had accepted the offer!

With only a few weeks until "closing", it was important that we had all our "ducks in a row". Some of the money I was to obtain from Mike's "Buy out" of the house, was to be used as down payment, but suddenly, Mike decided that he was going to *sell* the house and split the money rather than *keep it* and buy me out. Not to worry though, the LORD was still in control!

Mike placed a sign out in the yard: "House: For Sale By Owner" along with our home phone number. While I was there at our "house to be sold" one day, a man called our home phone, interested in this house for sale. Mike wasn't there, so I took a message for him. He had been handling the details of the "sell", so I left the information on his desk.

When Mike returned that evening, he found the printed note and headed up the stairs with it clinched in his hand. As he flung opened the door to the upper floor, he entered the kitchen inquiring, "What is this?" holding the note in the air, angrily. "It's a man that wants to look at the house whenever you can show it to him. He wants you to call him to set up a time." I told him.

"Let me get this straight," he said even more frustrated looking than before, "a man named "***Jesus***" wants to look at the house as a potential buyer." He was standing, shaking the note in disbelief. I answered calmly. "Yes, that's right.' Mike flung his arms up in the air in surrender . . ." Oh, man, I give up. I cannot believe this."

It was truly amazing. The man *did* show up to look at the house, but was not the person that ended up buying it. A family from out-of-state was the purchasers.

The Broker's Title Agency that handled *my* closing was the same one *Mike's* agent was using, but not by our choosing or knowledge. Our realtors had no idea of what they had done when they scheduled the closing of Mike's new home, at the *same place* and *same time* as mine. When the agency realized what they had done, they purposefully placed us in separate rooms, quite a distance apart. I assured them all the "extra effort" was unnecessary, but they were apologetic and thoughtful as this kind of "permanent separation" is usually a time of *hard feelings* for most couples.

After the official "closings" were completed, Mike and I said our goodbyes out in the parking lot. We hugged each other and went in totally opposite directions. His home was off of Highway 33 East and ours was off of Highway 33 West.

When I arrived at our new home, I was alone. The realtor was to soon be delivering the keys. With the feeling of relief, I walked along the driveway and took a look at the rich chartreuse green grass in the front yard. Exhausted from this emotional and "trying" day, I sat, and then stretched out on my back, underneath our property's two huge trees. As I stared upward towards the sky, the branches and leaves of Majestic Oaks swayed back and forth. It was as if they were waving to welcome me, after my very long journey home.

Chapter Thirty-four

Just Ask!

And I say unto you; Ask, and it shall be given you; seek, and ye shall find; knock, and it shall be opened unto you. Luke 11:9

In a matter of days since the move, the children and I had painted the walls and hired someone to lay carpet through the floors of our new home. Furniture was being placed in its "right spots" and things seemed to be coming together. As we unpacked the boxes marked "fragile", I found it quite a change to be able to place some of my Christian "trinkets" on the shelves. Before, such things were frowned upon when we lived on Bridle Court. At this home though, we were even able to hang one of those pictures of Jesus by Warner Sallman in our living room. It had been stored in my parents' attic for years.

As I looked around the almost completed front room, I thought, "There is something missing here." I remembered that I'd seen in someone's home before, a Family Bible on a coffee table laid opened. If I had to say what the finishing touch to our new home would have been; *that* would have been *it*.

Over the next week, I began to check into what different retailers had to offer on their Family Bibles. To my surprise and discouragement, the price of them, at the very least was $50.

So, I left my request with the LORD about the "finishing touch" I'd desired, and put it to the bottom of my priority list.

After work one morning, I was on my way home, when I realized, "its Saturday!" Working "overnights" sometimes caused my days and nights to run together. During the summer months, I'd had a tendency to get "carried away" with chasing down yard sales on weekends, and I had begun to limit myself to just a few. So on that morning, starting out from my workplace, I warned myself, "You can only go to the ones you find between here and the house." Yep, sometimes one finds one talking to themselves after pulling a 10 hour shift while fighting sleep.

About two blocks from where I'd begun, as I traveled along High Street, I spotted the corner house with the people out front . . . "Yes; a yard sale!" I banged the steering wheel with happy hands; parked and flung the door open like a "madwoman". Approaching the owners of the items slowly, I smiled a warm "Mornin'" hoping to hide the "yard sale junky" that lived inside of me. Strolling with a calm appearance to their "goods", I feasted my eyes on some candles. "Like I don't have enough candles, I thought", but picked them up to "smell" anyway.

There were baby items and picture frames, clothes and trinkets galore, but as I walked, I passed it all by, thinking I must be cured. I had almost completed my "run" of the place, when something caught my eye. There on the very last table, lay a huge leather book, burgundy with gold letters on the side. I walked quickly over and picked up the treasure. It was heavy and quality made.

Halving the book between my hands, I opened it to find God's Word. "It's a Bible!" I excitedly gasped, as I found its first page to see. "King James Version" was printed inside the cover and it had an empty section for a family tree!

There were pictures I'd never seen before; history and artifacts in the back. I was thrilled but then I hesitated for a moment: "It must be priced very high." Closing the book, I began to look on the binding and outside for a label. It wasn't until I turned it over to the back that I spotted the marking: **$ 1.00**

Nothing that you have not given away

will ever be really yours.

C.S. Lewis

Chapter Thirty-five

Beautiful

But the LORD said unto Samuel,
Look not on his countenance, or on the height of
his stature; because I have refused him: for the
LORD seeth not as man seeth; for man looketh on
the outward appearance, but the LORD looketh
on the heart. I Samuel 16:7

After being married for 13 years, it was difficult to be alone again, and know just how to feel about myself; For a woman who takes on the last name of someone, and becomes intertwined with that mate, experiences a violent jolt when awakened one day to find only half of herself present. After all, you see yourself through another's eyes, and their perception of you becomes yours. Note to self: It is never good to hang all your worth on what someone constantly tells you; whether it is good or bad.

During the last few weeks Mike and I were together, he had used hurtful words and negative comments to tear me down. He made sure I knew that I was unattractive and unwanted.

By this time, I was working an "overnight shift" at a Healthcare facility and taking a psychology class at the local Community College. I was trying desperately to get my life back on track, minus one.

As I visited the restroom while at work on this particular night, I caught a glimpse of myself in the mirror. I looked at the person staring back at me and had several thoughts. I began to talk to the LORD, as I turned away. "I really don't need anyone but You, Lord. I just feel so ugly sometimes."

It was nearing the end of my shift so I made one last check on the status of the residents. I heard my "replacement staff" make their way in and we chatted a couple of moments while I gathered my things to leave. As I entered the parking lot to walk to my car, I continued my conversation with the Lord. "Is it really too much to ask to have someone show me the same kind of love that I give to others?" Tearing up by now, I whispered, "How do people see me, Lord? Am I really as repulsive as Mike acts like I am?"

When I left work at 9am, I stopped by Food Lion for a few things. I went there a lot for milk, bread and such because it's just around the corner from "work" and on the way home. The store never really seemed to be crowded.

I strolled the isles leisurely, looking for the items I'd need to make Potato-Beef Soup. I'd worked my last "overnight" for a few days and wanted to make something warm and comforting to fill my family's stomachs. Heading toward the back of the store, on the way to the "Meats", I saw a man that I'd seen before working that department. This morning, he happened to be unloading a cart of reduced "burger". He smiled as he always did, as I got closer. "Hi. How are you today?" he asked. "Fine, how are you?" I replied in such a quiet voice, that I wasn't sure he'd heard. The man took a few steps my way and said, "My name is Alex. And your name is?" I responded, "LuAnn". He extended his hand to shake mine and continued. Placing his hand over his heart and then looking kind of confused, he said, "I want you to know that I'm not a pervert or anything, and I don't know why I'm telling you this," . . . He lifted up his hands in question, "but I've seen you in here before, and I have to say . . ." . . . "I just wanted to tell you . . . that I think you're a beautiful woman." I could feel my face burn red, displaying my embarrassment. Suddenly I realized that the LORD had spoken through this man, and I grinned and then stumbled for the words, "Thank you so much, that was very nice of you to say . . . I have noticed *your* smile also." Still seeming confused at his own forwardness, he said, "What?" and I repeated what I'd said, trying to not show how "shaken" I was. "Do you have any ground beef that's reduced?" I quickly changed the subject. He assured me he did, and offered a look at it, as it lay on the cart. I didn't see the portion size I'd needed, so I walked to the regular section of ground beef. He watched me as he worked, and noticed where I was, "Oh, get what you want and I'll mark it down for you." Still red-faced, but trying to remain "cool", I spoke, "But these meats have just been packed; you don't reduce them till much later, right?" "Oh, yes, I'll take whatever you pick out and make the reduction for you." I picked out just over a pound of the burger in the case and he slashed the price on what I had chosen, then before I left, he asked, "what was your name again?" as if he'd just snapped out of a 'state'. I answered his question with, "LuAnn" then, smiled, turned and said, "Thanks, Alex".

When I left that store, I could not wipe the grin off my face! The Lord had given me exactly what I'd asked for! As I hopped in the car that cold winter morning, I pulled down the mirror to see what the poor confused man had seen. Laughing at myself I made the statement, "I can't become vain on this one, Lord." My graying hair, although styled twisted up was looking a little scraggly from the night before. I had no makeup on my face or on my sleepy morning eyes and underneath a puffy white coat; I wore tennis shoes and a skirt. The sweatshirt that I definitely favored was adorned with cat hairs from holding a cat at work the night before. But its lettering spelled out all I wanted to say that day, "JESUS, That's My Final Answer."

I don't know whether this man loved Jesus or was just a vessel for Him to use that day, but I will never forget how the Lord heard my cry and let me know just how *He* sees me . . . and that's "Beautiful"!

Chapter Thirty-six

Okay, Lord, You Win

But whoso hath this world's good, and seeth his brother have need, and shutteth up his bowels of compassion from him, how dwelleth the love of God in him?
My little children, let us not love in word, neither in tongue; but in deed and truth. I John 3:17–18

It was May of 2003. Joshua had only been 18 for a month. "Man, is he 18 already?" I thought. "Well, yea . . . 1985, 90, 95, 2000 and 3 more; yep, he *is*." It's tough, I'm sure on every mother, to realize that you won't have your children small and dependant forever. Hey, we don't even *live* forever. Well, not in "this skin" anyway.

Joshua, *my* son had been working for a "cleaning company" for quite a while. I'd almost gotten used to the crazy hours and multiple places he had to go, to complete what he'd been assigned. I remember, while he only had his "driver's permit", I would ride with him in his car from job to job and sleep in the vehicle while he cleaned. Working "overnights" was tough when trying to survive on "small increments of sleep" in a hot car during the day.

One Sunday, at church, an announcement came over the "mic", "I don't know how many of you have had a chance to meet Brother Carlos. He's been visiting with us for a while now . . . Brother Carlos is looking for some men to help in his busy painting business. He's paying $7.00 and hour . . . is that right, brother?" A tall thin man sitting on the left side of the sanctuary nodded as the pastor continued. "Yes, he's paying $7.00 and hour for anyone who has time to help and wants to make some extra money."

By that time, Joshua was driving alone. He had been very responsible handling the hectic schedules and extra filthy locations assigned to him. After church, Joshua was all over me with, "Mom, did you hear that? The new man, Brother Carlos needs help painting. I'm going to call him and ask him when I can start." "What? I responded, "Oh, no. Joshua, you are NOT going to be climbing up and down on ladders up against some huge house somewhere." "Ma! Come on! I know I can do this! It won't be dangerous! I won't get hurt. It's just paintin' Ma." Joshua pleaded. "Josh . . . that Brother Carlos might have you climbing up on roofs or something. I don't want to take a chance on you getting hurt." Joshua knew his limits on pushing me. He knew this discussion was over . . . . for now anyway.

One day, Sister Crowley and I had lunch at Taco Bell. We met there quite often to sit and talk and to eat, of course. I loved their Bean Burritos and Chalupas. When we had taken our seat in my favorite booth, we said a quick prayer over the meal. We both unwrapped our special orders while the conversation began. "Hey, LuAnn," she spoke first and quietly, as if she had a secret to share. "Have you seen that guy, Brother Carlos at the church?" I tilted my head a bit, and answered "uh-huh"; I had just taken the first bite of my lunch. "Well, did you know that HE has been through stuff like you have?" she asked, as I dipped my chalupa in Fire Sauce and took another bite. Grimacing at the 'heat' in my mouth and thought of what she'd said, I swallowed, then asked, "Oh, yea? Like what?" "Well, his wife, she told him she didn't love him or want him anymore. He's been going through it pretty rough." My face wore a sympathetic look as I halted my dips and chewing. "Are you serious? Oh. That's so sad." I paused and sat, imagining how he must feel, then commented, "I *did* notice he was hunched over quite a bit during the service Wednesday night. He looked very sad or kind of 'beaten down'. Sister Crowley, after listening, went on, "He's got two little girls and she won't let him see them. He *is* really down and needs our prayers". "Oh, my" I added, "I wonder why he can't see his girls. No wife and now his daughters? The situation *is* really bad." Sister Crowley's 'fixer' attitude took charge then, as she announced, "And he's thin as a rail; he needs a belt too!" I laughed at her comment of observation, and the conversation soon went to other matters.

Sunday morning came, and before I went to my class, I shoved a bag underneath Sister Crowley's seat. "This is a belt for you to give Brother Carlos and a CD with some songs that helped me when I was low. Don't dare let anyone know I got it for him. It's from *your* family, agreed?" She smiled and said, "Awuh" as she peeked in the bag, then shoving it back under her chair to give him later.

Meanwhile, Dad and Mom had planned a trip to come and visit us in Virginia. They wanted me to make a list of anything I needed help with. I fussed, because I told them I just wanted to "spend time with them". I really didn't want them to work while they were there. Back when we'd first bought the house on Rockingham Drive, they'd come up and done a whole "slew" of things around our house. They promised to "not do so much" this go-round.

The weekend came, they arrived and "right to work" they went. One of the jobs on the "short list" was that Dad wanted to replace some blown off shingles and help me put a screened top onto the house's gutter system. He reasoned, "That way, the leaves won't get into them and stop them up."

"Okay, okay, Dad, I'll be your assistant, but I don't want to get on top of the house!" When it came time to flush out the already leaf stuffed gutters, we tried it with Dad up top and me on a ladder, but it didn't seem to be working too well. I was scared of heights and my Dad suggested, "Why don't you let Josh come up here and help me." "Oh no; BIG mistake", I thought, as I saw a smile cross Joshua's face. "Come on, Mom. Paw Paw needs me to help. Ain't nuthin' gonna happen to me." Wearing his sweet smile and looking at me with those handsome brown eyes, my son was plenty convincing. With a sigh of defeat, I conceded to them both, "Al-right. But you'd better be careful".

Dad and Joshua worked well as a team that day as they cleaned, repaired and installed. My Mother and I stood in the front yard watching, as they labored in the hot sun. During a break they were taking, we served them tall glasses of iced water. While they sat and lay atop the roof, in almost a teasing kind of way, I looked up and captured the moment on camera. As I moved the device away from my eye, I whispered, "Okay, Lord . . . . You win." And I knew that I had to let my son go. Joshua was going to work for that Brother Carlos.

Chapter Thirty-seven

Son & Fun

For I know the thoughts that I think toward you, saith the LORD, thoughts of peace, and not of evil, to give you an expected end. Jeremiah 29:11

It was 4:30 am. I was at work, running a fever. I felt like I couldn't breathe. I was worried that I may have passed this "stuff" onto Joshua, my son, not knowing I was sick the night before. As I sat, trying to "make it through the rest of my shift I thought of yesterday's events.

Joshua had come home that Tuesday evening, after painting all day with the man from our church, Brother Carlos. He'd also finished up the cleaning at his other job for Brother Driver. He began to share his day with me as I "wound down" planning to sleep. His excitement was incredible for that late hour. "Mom, Brother Carlos and I, we pray before we start work everyday, and he's been teaching me how to paint inside and out." "That's so good, Josh" I said, as my eyes became heavy, and my speech a little slurred from lack of rest. "Today Brother Carlos said my name while I was painting, and when I turned my head to see what he wanted, his paintbrush hit my face." Joshua was laughing as he explained. "Then, I took *my* paintbrush and chased him around the yard, trying to get him back!" Laughing wearily with him, I responded, "I'm glad you are learning and having fun doing it, son. That's ya'll pray too!"

As he mocked my slurred responses in our conversation, he knew that I was about to "fall out", Joshua attempted to keep me awake and began to show me some "defense moves" he'd recently learned, using me as his guinea pig. As many times before, I said, "Oh, Josh, I'm so sleepy." I could hardly hold my own head up at that moment, much less attempt to "defend myself" against his simulated attacks.

"Come on Ma ..." he responded, as he tried to show me how to "get away from" someone that had their arm around my neck from behind. I think I kind of surprised him, when I sunk my teeth into his forearm and used my short nails to "give him a scratch", for he jerked away and bumped my nose in the process; we both yelped and laughed. As he returned to give me another "dose", he held both my arms so that I couldn't move. I tried and tried to get away from him, but instead of conceding, I thought of a way to escape. Just like a baby does when they don't like the taste of their food, I began to "Whine, blow and spit" in his direction. Josh was so shocked, that the sight of his wide eyes made me laugh harder. As he held his grip more determined than before, I "whined, blew and spit" again. The force was so hard that it blew my hair back away from my face and Joshua began to fight the same way. Our guts were hurting so badly from laughing, that neither of us had strength left to fight.

Taking a "breather", we continued to talk, but about more serious things. He told me that when he finishes college and makes some "great money" he would take care of me. He teased me about putting me in a Nursing Home in my "old age" and after he'd gotten his laugh, assured me I'd come live with him.

As I grew more tired, my voice became hoarse, and I cleared my throat a few times. Josh mocked the small noise I'd made and told me I needed to do it like his "Paw Paw". He demonstrated my dad's famous "throat clearing gesture", "Bhur-ur-ur-ur!" with the instruction to let my lips be a little looser. We both "cracked up" hearing "Paw Paw's" noise, as I completed the task with perfection. It doesn't take much to "get someone started" when they're delirious from lack of sleep. As I crawled in my bed, dropping hints for my son that it was time to leave me alone, his "picking mood" had not left him yet. He took my covers and lifted them up, bringing them towards my head and neck. I thought he was going to pretend to smother me, but instead tucked the covers around my neck. I reminded him that I was a "mommy" and not a "mummy" as he continued to tuck me in. After he'd finished, he said, "Goodnight Mama." with a smile and turned off my lights. I believe I slept the best that night that I had in a long time.

Chapter Thirty-eight

God Shall

But let the righteous be glad; let them rejoice before God: yea, let them exceedingly rejoice. Psalm 68:3

I continued to have a fever and cough. I usually could "ride it out" when I got a little sick, but something was different about this 'cold'. It just wouldn't go away. I worked until I could hardly breathe, and then finally gave in. I had not needed to visit Rockingham Family Physicians facility in quite a while, and because my visits had been far apart, I'd always gotten a different physician each time I had gone.

"Hello? Yes, I need to see one of your doctors, as soon as possible, I'm afraid. I have a cold that just won't go away. I feel weak and have been coughing a lot." After giving her all my information she paused a few seconds as she was looking for a spot. "Alright" the voice on the other line said. "Can you come in at 11 today?" I told her that was fine.

I got off work at 9 am that morning, and needed to stay awake for the appointment. I sluggishly drove to my friend, Sister Crowley's, so that she would keep me company while I waited. Sister Crowley was not only a friend, but a mentor to me. She had been serving the LORD for many years. I, on the other hand, had only returned to Him 7 years ago. When we would get together, many times, I would quiz her on subjects pertaining to God's Word. This morning, sleepy or not, it would be no different. "Sister Crowley, I know it's a strange question, but if we really want God's Will, why do we pray? Why don't we just let things be? My friend took a deep breath asking for wisdom, and began to speak to me. "LuAnn, we are supposed to desire God's highest Will for us. We ask for things, like certain jobs, a house or to be healed. And that's communication with the LORD. He wants us to talk to Him." I sat totally into what she was teaching me. "Remember the scripture about 'Ask and ye shall receive; Seek and ye shall find'?" I nodded, rubbing my tired eyes. "And the Lord's Prayer is the perfect example of *how* we *should* pray" she added. Sister Crowley went on to explain how our lives were like an intertwined tapestry. "Each life, yours, mine and everyone's crosses over each other's; God sees everything as "present", not like we see today, or tomorrow." He has already worked everything out just the way it's supposed to be. That's why we shouldn't fret. Remember: *Luke 12:22-34* and *Matthew 6:34* gives us explanations of why we should not worry so much! When we want what the LORD wants for us, all is taken care of." *Jeremiah 29:11-13 For I know the thoughts that I think toward you, saith the LORD, thoughts of peace and not of evil, to give you an expected end. Then shall ye call upon me, and ye shall go and pray unto me, and I will hearken unto you. And ye shall seek me, and find me, when ye shall search for me with all your heart.* and *Romans 8:28 And we know that all things work together for good to them that love God, to them who are the called according to his purpose.*"

Matthew 6:34 Take therefore no though for the morrow: for the morrow shall take thought for the things of itself. Sufficient unto the day is the evil thereof.

"So when we pray, for ourselves or our friends, it's to show Him how much we care. If you had a Father, a Brother or a Friend and never talked with him, wouldn't that be sad?" The LORD loves it when we come to Him with our needs, no matter how great or small. It's sad to say, but some people don't even take the time to talk to Him until they do need something." My head dropped. "I don't want to be like that, Sister Crowley." She smiled, as I had listened to her wonderful explanation. I wanted to make sure that I understood it correctly. "So, when we ask, He already knows what we are going to ask for?" I threw my arm up over my mouth and coughed hard. The rattle sounded deep. "Yes LuAnn. He already knows."

We prayed that morning before I left for my appointment, but mostly just to thank the LORD for His Goodness, for our fellowship time and for His Word and Holy Spirit who leads, guides and teaches us.

Time had passed quickly, as we talked about 'heavenly things'. Soon, it was 10:40 am, and with a thankful heart, I bid my friend goodbye. "I'm praying you feel better soon, LuAnn." Sister Crowley said, as I opened my car door to get in. "Thank you, friend." I responded; I closed the door and drove away.

While reading the Good Housekeeping magazine in the waiting room, I began to nod off; after all, I'd worked 10 hours, stayed up a couple more and was running a fever by this time.

"LuAnn Turner", the sound of my past married name being announced across the room jabbed and startled me at the same time. I pulled myself up, and followed the woman in the uniformed smock down the hall to a room. It was only a few moments before a young doctor in a white lab coat came in with a clipboard. "So, LuAnn, tell me what's going on with you today?" After explaining my symptoms, and letting him know that I hardly ever get sick, he listened to my chest and looked down my throat. "Are you allergic to any medications, Mrs. Turner?" "No." I said, taking the "name hit" again. "Alright, then, I'm writing you a prescription for Cephlaxin; it's generic for Keflex. You have a touch of Bronchitis. Take the medicine and get some rest. Do you have to work today?" he inquired. I could hardly keep up with his instructions and questions. It's not that he talked fast or anything. It's that I was exhausted. "No. I'm off for the next 2 days." "Alright, then; Follow the instructions on your medicine and call me if you have questions or concerns." "Okay. Thanks so much." I replied, just ready to find a couch or bed somewhere to lie down on. As I left the facility, I dreaded the wait I was going to have to endure at the Walmart Pharmacy; but at least it was located right across the street from the doctor's office.

"It'll be about 30 minutes" the young woman taking my prescription slip and information told me. I walked around the store a bit. "I can stay awake as long as I keep walking" I thought to myself. Walmart definitely has enough 'stuff to look at' to occupy at least 3 hours of one's time; but again, it didn't take that long. "Thank you!" I picked up my 'drugs' when they were ready and headed to my car. "Where did I park again?" I wandered like a zombie through the lot. "I know it was on the pharmacy-side entrance. Oh. There it is." Now, it doesn't take a sleepy person to loose their vehicle in a Walmart parking lot, so don't *even* act like you haven't done it.

"Ahhhh" I sighed, as I sat in the seat behind the steering wheel. "Home, James!" I humorously commanded my car." I felt a relief of the burdensome morning coming to an end. "Oops, before I drive off, let me take my medicine, so I won't suddenly forget when I see my bed." I opened the white bag stapled with folded instructions on it; Fumbling with the plastic brown bottle, I pushed down on the cap and twisted it off. Tilting it a bit to allow a pill to slide out, I popped it into my mouth and proceeded to take a sip from the "Deer Park water" my friend had given me that morning. Suddenly, in my "groggy" state, I realized that I hadn't read the instructions. "Oh! Was I supposed to take one pill or two?" I'd been thinking of my earlier conversation with Sister Crowley and was having trouble concentrating. Sitting right there in my little green Saturn, on the busy lot of Walmart, I stopped what I was doing to pray. "Lord, *if* it be Your Will to have this medicine make me well again, please have it do so; In Jesus Name I ask You, Amen." As I brought the bottle of pills up to get a closer look at the instructions, I immediately received the answer to my prayer:

"GOD SHALL"

You see, in my weariness, sickness and confusion, I hadn't even bothered to check out my doctor's name. It was none other than Stephen E. Godshall, M.D.

Chapter Thirty-nine

Our 'On Time' & 'Online God'

Cast thy bread upon the waters: for thou shalt find it after many days. Ecclesiastes 11:1

The children and I stayed pretty busy with our jobs, church and friends. I had continued to work on the house, making improvements. I had finally made my way to the "outside".

While the children went off to "Youth Convention" I planned out how to spend each day. When the children arrived home, the house surely had changed; it was not white but tan. It had taken me a few hours each day to climb the 24 foot ladder and complete the job, but I had just loved the color of the Crowley's house, and had visualized ours like theirs. I love "challenges" and this had been a big one. It's always fun to "see a project or challenge through". But *that* venture brings to mind one thing I had visualized and planned . . . . but had *not* "followed through" on. Let me explain.

Back when the children and I were at the Nazarene Church, they needed money to expand. While sitting comfortably at their "fundraising formal dinner", I listened intently to the message at hand. The thought of more room, more seats and more souls saved, through this outreaching "Beacon Of Hope", made me think long and hard about "giving". The printed cards that lay on our tables, asked for one donation, or a commitment for a year. I pondered which would be the better choice for me; what my budget, my finances could stand.

"I'm going to take it home and pray about it" I thought as the dinner was coming to its end. I spent the next week, pondering and praying over what the Lord would have me to give.

Around the same time, I had paid off my car, and had been thinking of trading it in for a larger model, but the nearest Saturn dealership was a couple of hours away in Winchester. I found out that "Saturn" had a website on the computer, and so I made time to get on the internet, and look them up. I was surprised to find, that you could now build your own, in a simulation, and order it online! Suddenly, the thought entered my mind, "Why not build one, and see what it would cost; and instead of ordering a vehicle for myself; give for a year, the difference in the new payment from the old payment to the church!"

I checked each box precisely as I build my very own car. Green outside, tan inside, power windows, CD player, and a "stick shift" to enjoy the sport of the ride. I ordered the L200 model that was larger than the one I'd been driving. My reasons for that were: the children had grown a lot and of course, more room means more comfort.

Taking the payments from an amortization table, and subtracting my old payment, I filled in the difference on the card marked "Building Fund" from the church. One year, at this amount each month for my "visualized car".

I took one last look at the picture of the Saturn, as I rolled the mouse to X out of the screen. I was so thankful that the Lord had helped me with this ingenious plan, and during that year, He blessed me with the monthly money to pay.

Now getting this story back to the present tense: while we were living on Rockingham Drive, remember? I'd just painted the house and all, I saw the mailman driving off one day and assumed that the mail had come. I walked down our thick blacktopped driveway to the box marked 250. Pulling the small stack of envelopes out, then shutting up the plastic door, I checked out what had come. "Bill, bill, oh, letter! Bill . . . oh, what's this?" As I opened the long somewhat thick piece of mail, an advertisement and offer revealed itself; it had one of those little fake keys attached with glue. "Win a gift card, win a thousand dollars, or win a car! Yea, right." I said sarcastically. "Well, I *am* going to Taco Bell today; I might as well stop by that "Charlie Obaugh place"; it's on the way." I rationalized. Who *wouldn't* take a chance on getting something free, if it 'happens to be' so convenient to do so?

My Saturn was about 5 years old and it had just reached that "mileage mark", that if I had planned to trade or sell, it was time. "But, "shoot", I may just win a couple of dollars or a car if I go. It's not going to cost me anything to try, right?"

Later, I found myself walking into the dealership, almost embarrassed at this "lame" attempt to get something free. But the sales people were nice, and I guess it was worth the effort, because I needed some "nice" that day.

I gave a gentleman my little fake key and told him I'd received it in the mail. He asked me just to have a seat at first; I did, as he wanted to talk for a while. He asked me if I was interested in buying a car and I told him that I just came by to see if I'd won anything with my key. He was a funny and easy-going man, and he obliged my request right away. I hadn't won a car, or cash or a card, but thanked him as I politely turned to leave. The thought entered my mind, since they had lots of used cars, to inquire of any Saturns they might have. "Well, I believe that there are two on the lot, let me see, you want automatic or "stick"?" he asked. Of course, my answer *was* "a stick" as he pulled the key to the car on the lot off the board.

I checked out that black Saturn. It looked good from the outside; it was the sporty model they made. But I had become attached to that *Green* on my '98 model and didn't know if I could see myself in a different color. I had just turned down the fancy little car, and had bid the salesman, "goodbye", when out of curiosity, I asked another question, "What color was that automatic you have?" He quickly answered and said, "Oh, it's over here." We strolled a few feet from where we had been and there it was: Big and GREEN. I smiled and took a few moments to examine what I'd just seen.

The more I looked, the more I questioned: "What year, how many owners, how much?" I knew better than to "imagine myself having it" because it causes one to act desperately and mess up. After a lengthy test drive with him, we went to the "table" for the figures and such. Back and forth, back and forth, he took offers and conditions to his boss. I was there for a couple of hours before we settled and signed papers. And THEN, . . . the 2002 Green, L200 model Saturn became *mine*!

Coming away with a "sweet deal", I grinned and was quite tickled at the "find". As I drove away in it, and hit some stoplights, I admired my new sweet ride.

"Look at that nice tan interior", I said, as I played with the buttons on the dash. Now, I could actually begin to enjoy it, since everything had been signed, settled and paid. The more I drove, the more I pondered, "Why does this car seem so familiar?"

Several days later, as I was driving down "Port Road", I spotted the huge, the expanded, the Beacon of a church. It hit me. I had my answer.

And what had happened brought back to mind what my Mother always used to say: **No matter how you try; you just can't "out-give" God.**

Reputation is

what men and women think of us;

Character is

what God and the angels know of us.

Thomas Payne

Chapter Forty

The Superman 'Knockdown'

Blessed are ye that hunger now: for ye shall be filled. Blessed are ye that weep now: for ye shall laugh. Luke 6:21

It was a typical, yet "Powerful" morning at Christ Gospel Church. As a "mother", I was so content. My daughter was singing on the Worship Team, my son, helping with the soundboard in back.

They were both happy and serving the Lord. I'd found it so true what many say, "It takes a village to raise a child", because there were lots of folks who had helped Joshua and Kathy along, teaching them what was important; what was right. After service that day, I was overwhelmed with gratitude for those that the Lord had recently sent our way. I made it a point to search out the "Brother Carlos", the man Joshua had been painting for.

People were scattered about just after "dismissal", and I spotted the tall man near one of the old shellacked doors. I called his name over the noisy crowd and he began to take a few steps my way. "Yes?" he looked down at me with a questioning but pleasant face, "Did you call my name?" Extending my right hand across a row of sanctuary chairs, I told him, "I wanted to say thank you today". He still looked a bit puzzled as he politely stuck his large hand out, taking hold of mine with a firm grip. "Oh, sorry, I'm LuAnn, Josh's mom; I just wanted to say "thank you" that's all. I wanted to let you know how much I appreciate you letting him paint for you. He told me about you guys praying together before you get started. I think that's great too." His expression went from "confused" to "surprised" as it finally hit him, "Oh! So YOU are Josh's

Mom." I smiled nervously as we'd finished our handshake and said, "Yes. I'm so thankful that you're teaching Josh some good things. He really is in need of a *manly* Christian influence for I'm afraid he's with his sister and me most of the time."

"Oh, well, yes, he's quite a hard worker and really good kid" Brother Carlos added, still smiling. "Okay, well, you have a good day and thanks again." I added awkwardly, as I turned and waved, approaching the door. "Okay. You too." Brother Carlos said, still standing in the same place; with a hand in the air.

A couple of days later, I purchased my Saturn from Charlie Obaugh's. I'd heard, that Joshua had been hanging out with his boss that day, getting a sound system put into his vehicle. Since the installation was being done near the dealership I'd just left, I decided to stop by and see him. I drove onto the lot where Joshua and his boss had been. As I pulled up closer to the front door of the place, I spotted Brother Carlos coming out of the store. "Hi, Brother Carlos, is Joshua inside? I spoke loudly for he was several feet away. "Oh, no, sorry, he left just a few minutes ago, to clean, at his other job." he replied, as he walked over my way. "Aw. I wanted to show him the car I just bought." I said, a little disappointed he was gone. "I guess I can catch him at the house tonight" I remedied, as I looked up while his height blocked the sun. Brother Carlos must have noticed the strain I experienced while I was tilting my head, for he leaned down to the window, and placed his hands on its frame. When his face had gotten a little too near mine, he said, "Oh!" and backed up a bit, suddenly aware of how he had quickly invaded my space. Embarrassed, he spoke nervously, and said, "Sorry, he'll hate that he missed you. So, you got this today?" He looked at the Saturn a moment and said, "It's nice. Is it new? It looks like it is." I smiled and explained. Afterwards, I drove around for a bit, enjoying the Sunny day. That night, I was able to show my children the "new ride" we could take our long trips in, comfortably. They liked it and rode around with me some the next day.

The following weekend, on Saturday, our church had a picnic, out at Purcell Park in Harrisonburg. Lots of people "showed up" with food and sports equipment. While the ladies set up their fine side dishes and desserts, most of the children and men had begun planning which games to play.

Just prior to the meal, everyone accept the birds singing, were quiet in respect while we asked a blessing over the food. As people loaded their plates and began to find their seats, I was aware of where my children were. I glanced up and saw Joshua's boss sitting in the corner alone, under the shelter the church had reserved. Stepping over to my son, I whispered, "Don't let Brother Carlos sit by himself. You can ask him to sit over here if you want." I had to send my son, of course, to offer that invitation, though, so no teasing or rumors got started. I had been a single mother and did not want to be 'set up' or 'kidded' at all about some random man. I know what a "cupid" *I* am when it comes to "matchmaking"; I thought my friends may be the same way. Joshua walked over and invited his boss to share a bench at the picnic table with us without drawing much attention to the situation; Brother Carlos seemed to be a little more at ease than the last time I saw him.

It didn't take long for folks to "down" the tasty food and run out to start the activities they'd chosen. There was football, volleyball, and walking the track; a variety for all ages and genders present. *I* wanted to participate in a basketball game that was taking place a short distance away from the crowd.

My sisters and brothers in Christ all stood round as we separated ourselves into teams. It had been a while since I'd shot "hoops" but I was among friends and was "pumped" to play.

Sister Duckworth was the tallest of the ladies, along with Sister Wilcox, but they were on different teams. And although Sister Thurman and I were the short ones in the crowd, we were jumpy and quick on our feet. Most of us ladies had our denim skirts on, as we dribbled and guarded our opponents. That did not keep us from being aggressive. Our strong wills to win gave us spunk.

Laughter and grunts could be heard as shots were made and stray balls were chased, but I saw that Brother Carlos was doing a little too well; So I waved my arms in his face; knowing he was on the opposing team, I was trying to prevent him from making his shots. I kept my hands up and guarded him like a pro, but suddenly, his determined and "driving" force, stole my balance. Skidding forward on my hands, torso and knees, all STOPPED and gasped in concern. It was told by observers that I jumped up, brushed off and said simply, "Come on, let's play ball!"

What I remember is the pain that I had felt as my knees and chest had hit the court. Ouuuuch!

Later, after the end of the game, on the walk back to the picnic site, I leaned with one arm on the shoulder of a "sister", then grabbed my right breast inconspicuously, with the inside of my arm. "Are you alright?" she laughed, looking around. "Oh, I hurt it right here when I fell, but I couldn't grab it in front of all those men." "Ahh . . . ouuuwie." I moaned and placed my arm to my chest. We both "cracked up" at the price I'd paid, for acting like I was some young Michael Jordan.

Later, two or three of us ladies helped the kids fill up some miniature balloons with water for a secretly planned "water balloon fight". We had so much fun splashing around and filling them at of the Park's fountain! High pitched screams and laughter interrupted the rhythmic bouncing of balls and squeaks of "swing chains" that were swaying back and forth. Playful youngsters were scampering all about as their clothes and hair were becoming soaked.

With a milking pail full of bouncy, colorful ammunition, we began scooping out the fat balloons by the handfuls. Like athletes with "shot-puts", going for the Gold we aimed and pushed forward at our targets. Since most of the church folks were ducking for cover, I figured no one would notice which direction *I* went. I put my "sights' on the "*new* kid of the church" (Brother Carlos), and bombarded him with a red, green, then blue! My smiles and laughter immediately ceased and my eyes looked up in fright. I saw that each balloon I'd thrown had not busted but amazingly bounced off his chest. There I stood; helpless, but guilty in his sight. Frozen from fear and riddled with shock I quickly "snapped out of it" then took off for more. As I ran across the grassy path, I whispered in amazement at what I'd seen. "Those things sprung off him like bullets off *Superman*! Who *is* this man?" I was confused.

I didn't return to the site of the crime, but made myself scarce for a while; for the pail had been emptied, and all the water that was left, was on a bunch of drenched people, running around.

When the excitement calmed, I let Joshua and Kathy know I'd be leaving soon. They told me they'd see me back at the house later. There was a football game being planned as I exited a bathroom near the shelter. I had been talking with a friend, Charity, as we walked back toward the group. But was interrupted by another voice; "Hey, Charity! Are you going to play?" the Superman called out. Teams were being formed to play a football game. Inside I was somewhat disappointed that he had not spoken to me. "Oh, I don't know," she replied, "I think it's about time for me to "run"." She was like me, and worked a 3rd shift, and needed to sleep for the night ahead. She talked with me a few moments more, and I told her I was leaving too. "Alright," she said, "Well, have a nice sleep" and smiled, I bid her the same. I took one last look at my church family, in the thick grassy field, as they tossed the ball. I stole a quick glance at that "superman" guy, got in my car and drove away.

Chapter Forty-one

Rocks, Cat-hair & Fire-sauce

Not that which goeth into the mouth defileth a man; but that which cometh out of the mouth, this defileth a man. Matthew 15:11

A new quarter was beginning soon in our Sunday School Classes; that meant changing boards and décor. New inspiring pictures and messages hung, would parallel the next lessons to be taught.

Sister Driver, our Sunday School Superintendant, asked if I would meet her on Thursday; she wanted me to help paint a mural for the church hall. "Oh, yes, I love to paint", I replied. "I'm not real good at drawing, but I'll do whatever you want." Thursday came and she and I talked as we dipped our brushes. We filled in the trees, the birds and clouds. As we were finishing up with some "final touches"; she'd suggested I paint a few rocks in the grassy part of our mural. As I moved toward the bottom of the large scene, I made myself comfortable and sat cross-legged on the floor. From behind us, across the room, I heard someone open the side door. "Oh, hi Brother Carlos!" Sister Driver greeted, as he turned to close the huge door. Out of my peripheral vision I saw him take a seat on the bench by the entrance. "Hi Sister Driver", Brother Carlos replied. "I was just stopping by to check with the Reverend; He has some painting he wants me to do." Sister Driver was attentively listening to his words. "What are ya'll doing?" he threw the focus off himself and onto the colorful wall at hand. "Oh, Sister LuAnn and I were just completing this for Sunday School. Isn't that right, Sister LuAnn?" "Yes, that's right". I replied, not wanting to jump in and talk. "Well, what are you painting *there*, Sister LuAnn?" that Brother Carlos asked. "Rocks", I replied, with no other words to add. Awkwardly, she kept talking "Well, is it hot outside, Brother Carlos?" Sister Driver tried to continue the conversation with this painter man, and she did do a good job. But I wasn't *even* going to pretend I was interested in this man who "knocks women down in basketball", and "calls out "Charity's" name to play football". I didn't care if the balloons DID bounce off his chest. Reverend O'Haran walked in shortly after and took Carlos into his office.

Friday, Joshua, Kathy and I were invited to the Crowley's for pizza and some kind of charades. Our families had spent a lot of time together since we moved only 3 miles from them. We accepted the invitation excitedly. I was especially glad to have something to take my mind off the fool I'd made of myself the Saturday before at the park. What kind of nonsense . . . . Me: thinking of liking a man again? I was ashamed of the almost "girlish" feelings I'd had, while blocking that man's shots and throwing balloons at him. "How silly and childish I was", I scolded myself.

That night, when we arrived at the Crowley's neat and tidy home, we saw a couple of extra vehicles out front. Upon entering the house, we found they belonged to Carlos and Charity. "The more the merrier" I thought to myself, having come to the realization that Charity really deserved a husband, as she was in her mid 20s.

We all ate together, talked and laughed, but I noticed that Charity had gone outside. I looked and she was walking the yard, and talking on her phone. "How rude" I thought, as I rolled my eyes. I was angered by her obvious ingratitude and lack of consideration for this "Brother Carlos" man that had to have liked her. Suddenly I realized my judgmental spirit, I reprimanded myself harshly. "What is *wrong* with me", I thought afterwards. "It's not like I could ever *be with* this man. I must just be feeling protective or responsible for him." "Yea; THAT'S it. I just don't want him to be hurt again." I'd almost convinced myself of this thought, when I followed up on the reason Charity was outside.

I'd opened the front door and was making my way across the grass; coming towards this "young lady on the phone". "What are you doing?" I lipped, so not to disrupt her conversation. She smiled, but looked serious, as she returned to her connection. "I know, Mom, that's what I thought too". She was grinning at me and just kept talking, so I went back inside while she finished her call.

Later, Charity called me outside and told me that she had been on the phone with her mother. She went on to say, "Sister LuAnn, mom and I both agree, that YOU are the one that is supposed to be with Brother Carlos." "WHAAAAAAAAAT ?" I said, trying to hold back the huge grin inside my mouth. "Charity's mom lived all the way out in Florida; How could SHE possibly know what's going on up *here*?" I thought. I laughed nervously, trying not to show I cared. "What are ya'll saying? And where did you get such a *crazy* idea?" (I thought that was good enough to fool her) Then she explained how much the "painter man" and I had in common. I let my grin surface a bit, but did not dare allow myself to think it was possible. "Aw. Come on, let's go inside and play that game." I shrugged, and back to the crowd we went.

While passing out the game pieces and going over rules, Charity whispered to Sister Crowley. They both looked at me and then Brother Carlos and giggled like they had a plan in mind.

The game was going smoothly, and Brother Carlos was getting over his obvious shyness, when something about "cats" was mentioned in the game. This man, who'd said nearly nothing in the last hour, finally had something to say. "I don't really like cats in the house." Out of his big mouth it came. "Weee-ull", Sister Crowley let out her famous Southern drawl saying. Charity, Sister Crowley and I were bug-eyed and had to stop the game; we almost fell on top of one another laughing. You see, I had 2 *indoor* cats at home. Of all things Brother Carlos could have said; that was, by far, the most ironic and hilarious.

The rest of the night was fun and relaxing, knowing I was under no pressure, because after all, Brother Carlos didn't even like cats! Let me see, boyfriend, cats . . . . Boyfriend or cats . . . . It's a "no brainer" . . . . CATS WIN!! Ha!!

Sunday came. The mural Sister Driver and I had painted looked nice. And of course, the preaching and worship was just awesome that day!

Returning to church that night, for evening service, I was a little tired from lack of sleep. Sister Crowley told me that Brother Carlos had thanked them for the belt and CD. He'd actually worn the belt to church that day, but of course, *I* hadn't noticed.

After service was over, that man started walking my way. "I *know* he's not coming over *here*." My heart was racing . . . "What? Oh hi." Yep, he stopped right in front of me. "Hi, Sister LuAnn . . . um . . . I was wondering . . . um . . . you want to go, I mean, would you like to . . . um . . . get something to eat?" Seeing that I was about to slide under a seat uncomfortably red-faced, he looked past me and said, "And you too." He pointed at the Crowley family. "I mean, are ya'll hungry? I thought we could grab a bite to eat together." The Crowleys looked at each other and shook their heads negatively. They knew they could not go because of their "lack of funds". In a way, I was a little disappointed, but didn't show them. Suddenly, Brother Carlos added, "Oh, it's on me! Come on and go!" Brother and Sister Crowley were still hesitating, trying to be polite. I reached up and whispered in my friend's ear, "Why don't you accept his offer and then ask him to dinner next week in exchange?" It didn't take her a moment to respond: "Okay, we will go. But just as long as you come to eat with us next Thursday night." She said. He responded, "Yes! Of course! That'll be great!"

"Whew! That was a close one!" I thought. I don't know if I was more scared of saying no, when I really wanted to go, or that the Crowley's may turn him down and I'd have to make that decision quickly.

Once we arrived at Taco Bell, I was just fine! It was my very own comfortable place; the one I visited everyday. I'd spent hours studying there and even had my favorite booth. The employees called me by name that night and it brought a "relaxing" and "like home" kind of feeling. While in line, we found out that Brother Carlos had never been inside a Taco Bell. So in celebration for this special occasion, I thought I'd challenge him like on the basketball court, but with 10 fire sauces instead.

"Now I have to do what?" he asked, as we explained the new rules. "You have to eat at least 10 fire sauces with your meal tonight." Both families joined in to "cheer" us on. "Yea, 10 fire sauces! 10 fire sauces!" they shouted and laughed. "Well, we'll see about that", Brother Carlos said, as he asked the cashier for 12 with a 'smart' chuckle. Rolling my eyes followed by an "Oh, brother" was my response to his "big talk" and "confidence".

As we sat together in Taco Bell, as a church family, the night was the "best" I'd had in a long while. Brother Carlos was the center of attention, as he dipped his burrito in the red liquid mess on a wrapper. His face turned red and his top lip was sweating as he set out to accomplish his goal. We both ingested 11 fire sauces a piece that night, for one of the 12 had fallen in the floor.

The next week, Brother Carlos and I talked several times on the phone, and after 7 days had passed, we still had much to say. For only one week past the "Saturday evening Charades", we hit a record of a 5 hour overnight conversation.

At church the following morning, I peeped out the sanctuary swinging door. "He doesn't look *too* sleepy" I reported, for Sister Crowley heard about the night before. "Well, if he *is* sleepy, he *still* looks really happy!" I added jokingly, as I took one last peek. I pulled my head back into the hallway, grinning, and full of hope.

After church, Pastor Gus O'Haran and his wife were gathering their things and children too. They took Brother Carlos and me aside separately, and asked, "Why don't you join us for lunch?" Carlos and I both answered them, "Alright!" And on that day, we had an official "date" together for the very first time.

Chapter Forty-two

Everafter

Behold, how good and how pleasant it is for brethren to dwell together in unity! Psalm 133:1

It was a little strange for my son, Joshua, at first when his boss and I became close. After all, he was Joshua's friend first and now he was "dating his mom?" "Eewww! What was that all about?" But the LORD worked out the details; it didn't take long for all of us to adjust. And when we announced that we were planning to be married, Carlos asked Joshua to be his "Best Man".

So many folks in the church were involved in one way or another, in the planning of our wedding, whether it be volunteering services or blessing us with gifts. Here are just a few that stick out in my mind as I reminisce:

Sister Crowley arranged the beautiful flowers and purple and green colored reception.
Erin, another friend, offered to take photographs.
My family traveled all the way to Dayton, Virginia from North Carolina to attend, celebrating the day with us.
My sister and I ran around town finishing up last minute errands and getting my hair done.
Later, we met my parents, Brother and his wife, Shari at Luigis and talked while they ate.
Carlos' family came from Sperryville to be with us that day too!
My daughter, Kathy and some young girls from church helped me put on the finishing touches with my dress.

Daddy walked me down the isle to meet Carlos, Joshua and
Reverend O'Haran at the end.
I remember we lit a "unity candle" together as our sweet little friend,
Keturah sang the song: "Jesus Knows Me, This I Love";
its words were so special to me.

There were lots of surprises and great things that happened surrounding the moment we said our "I dos"; But the most AMAZING thing that happened that day took place at the end of the ceremony and reception:

Almost everyone was "in" on the surprise I'd planned for my new husband and his children. You see, Carlos loved horses, and had, most of his life. We had often times admired the Mennonites in town, with their horses and buggies. So I thought it appropriate, and quite a thrill to plan our own little excursion. Oh, what a dream it was! As the driver showed up in a black top hat and coat tails, we called everyone but "The Groom" and his children outdoors. Then we led Carlos out the door with his eyes closed. I picked up Samanda and he was carrying Samantha when the moment came for all to yell, "Surprise"! Carlos then opened his eyes. He was stunned as he took in this astonishingly beautiful sight. The humongous "Clydesdale Horses" shoulders were over 5 feet tall as they remained firmly on "all fours". The majestic animals stood strong while awaiting their tailored driver's commands.

My children had given their blessing ahead of time, as Samantha, Samanda, my husband and I were helped up onto the intricate and fairytale carriage while our guests snapped shots of the site. And as we rolled away down East View Street, it reminded us of our favorite movie, "EVER AFTER". Carlos said, "Let's wave! It's tradition!" As we turned to signal 'goodbye' to our family and friends, we heard the most amazing sound. "Is that coming from our church?" We asked. "Yes! Yes!" It was the church bell ringing!

I had wanted to have the bell rung that day, but had not told a soul of my desire. "Did you ask someone to ring it?" Carlos inquired, as we continued to wave back at the crowd left behind. "No! I thought YOU did!" I stated excitedly, "You mean you didn't?" We both laughed. We realized the LORD had truly smiled on us that day and any doubts of His blessing on us would be put to rest.

When we inquired, later, of the details of the bell we'd heard, we learned what had taken place that day. Joshua had been standing in the opened foyer of the church, watching us wave and ride away. Suddenly, a rope hanging from the ceiling caught his eye; he'd never noticed it before. Quickly, he realized what he was to do and reached up, pulled down with a 'tug'. We were informed after all was done, that the bell had not sounded in years. But on that chosen day and at precisely the right moment, its perfect ringing had pierced the air. "Dong . . . . Dong . . . Dong."

Chapter Forty-three

The Awesome Opportunity

If ye then, being evil, know how to give good gifts unto your children: how much more shall your heavenly Father give the Holy Spirit to them that ask him? Luke 11:13

Things were so NEW, as we began our life together. Many changes took place over the next 6 months. We bought a bigger home, our family spent time together and I was given a first shift position with PVI, Inc.

During that 6 month period, I was at my new job, one day, washing some dishes after feeding the clients there. A coworker, friend of mine had brought in another load of dishes to add to my pile from the lunchroom. She stopped and asked how things were going at home, being newly married and all. "Oh, everything's been great Kendra, but I just received a phone call from my daughter." I squirt a little more dishwashing liquid into the fading bubbled water. "I had recently told my daughter about a Nursing School opportunity at MTC." Kendra stood, watching me squeeze the long necked hose to create more bubbles, as I continued. "But . . ." I breathed a big sigh, "She says she doesn't' want to do go to school right now." My friend continued to listen with a sympathetic look. "This is an awesome opportunity for her. It costs only $1,500 for the first year and $2,000 the second. And after just 2 years, she'd walk away with a LPN license." I halted my whining and resumed my washing. My friend had a frank, matter-of-fact look on her face and asked, "Well, if it's *that* great of an opportunity, why don't YOU do it?" Now, Kendra was one that didn't mess around. She always said what was on her mind. "What?" I dropped the hose from my hand and stepped back, laughing.

"Yea sure; why don't *I* go?" I mimicked her words with a slight sarcasm. Kendra grinned and reaffirmed her thoughts. "I think you'd make a great nurse. So why do you laugh?" My heart was touched by her compliment and it had actually leaped in my chest at the thought of her suggestion. "I can't do something like that! I just got married 5 weeks ago!" I looked down at the remaining dishes to hide my excited smile. "Well, I think *you* should go. That's all I'm going to say." She ended. As I finished up the dishes, I couldn't shake the thought, the proposal, the chance that I could go back to school, and become a nurse.

Tomorrow would start the weekend, and although I could not get the wonderful suggestion out of my head, I decided to sleep on it before mentioning anything to Carlos. On Saturday, we'd decided to go for a bite at lunchtime. We usually used these times to 'catch up' on how our week had gone. When it was my turn to share my week, I let him know of a couple of serious matters and then, "Oh and I've got something *so* funny to tell you . . ." I turned red at the thought of Kendra's words as I repeated them aloud to him. Carlos was so receptive and encouraging, "Well, yea, LuAnn, you could! You could go back to school." I noticed his eyes looking to the table in deep thought. "I've always wondered what it would be like to be able to help people like that." He said, as his voice dropped. "Are you *serious?*" I asked, putting my hands under my knees as I leaned in from a seated position. "I didn't know that about you." As the conversation went on, we laughed and joked around about the possibility of us both attending school. We waited a couple of days, then checked into more of the details, and made an appointment to take the NET Test (Nursing Entrance Test). We both amazingly passed the test and began night classes on August 23rd, 2004.

We are the Bibles the world is reading;

We are the creeds the world is needing;

We are the sermons the world is heeding.

Billy Graham

Chapter Forty-four

Scattered Seeds

Owe no man anything, but to love one another:
for he that loveth another hath fulfilled the law.
Romans 13:8

The first year of school was filled with new and exciting things about anatomy and clinical procedures. Carlos and I continued to work our regular full time jobs as we plugged along in night classes. After several months of our crammed schedules, Carlos' boss began to give him a hard time over his priorities. He knew he was going to school at night, and decided to try to make him work extra late on his job. At the same time, we heard that the second year of school would only be offered during "daytime" hours. Carlos regrettably decided to quit nursing school. I felt bad about him not continuing, but found the answers to my "troubled spirit" quickly. "If Carlos had not begun classes, I would not have started either. It wasn't that I was afraid to go by myself, but I would not have taken a chance on placing a strain on our new marriage by doing that. So, you see, I saw God's Plan in the retrospect of things.

During the second year of school, Carlos began working for someone in our church. Reverend Prell co-owned <u>Select Field Services</u>, a local 'clean-out, foreclosure and maintenance business. Carlos was then able to allow me to put a "hold" on working for that school year, and concentrate fully on studies.

In May of 2006, I graduated from Massanutten Technical Center on the "A" honor roll. I couldn't wait to get back to work. But first, Carlos and I took a week's vacation to get away from everything; celebrating 2 years of hard work and our 2nd anniversary. Of all places we could have gone, we picked one very secluded; it was a Days Inn located in a remote area of Luray, VA. They were famous for their rooms with Jacuzzis. What a week of relaxation! And after that, it was time to GO TO WORK!

During the last couple of months of school, our instructors had given us pointers on the different aspects of our impending "job searches". I was "thrilled" at the idea that one day soon; I would have my first job as an official LPN.

We were encouraged to start applying for jobs around February and March prior to graduation. As I pondered on what *kind* of nursing I wanted to do, and the places I "visualized" myself working, I thought about the seeds that were scattered, in the story in Matthew 13, and how only some took root and grew. So, with the LORD as my guide, I collected many applications and filled them out over a period of a couple of days. On the day they had all been completed, I prayed the prayer, "Lord, I did my part, now You choose." Delivering each of the "apps" back to their facility, one at a time that day, I knew that, just like the seeds, falling on different "grounds"; one I'd casted would 'take hold' and eventually bear fruit.

When I had delivered the completed paperwork back to Avante, a woman told me I'd hear from someone closer to my graduation date. I was eventually able to interview with VMRC, and told I'd have a second interview with the Director of Nurses (D.O.N) because the first one had gone well. I awaited their call as instructed, but meanwhile, a woman named "Cori" phoned from Sunnyside; she set a time for us to talk later that week.

As I sat with Cori, from SPRC, I felt relaxed; at ease in her office. Afterwards, she took me on a tour of the large Retirement Community; it was beautiful, and had a large chapel to boot! Cori said, "LuAnn, I can see you working here", and I agreed, "I can see me working here too." I replied. We both laughed. She informed me that Ramona, their D.O.N. would not be back until the following week, so she couldn't officially offer me the position until Ramona gave the word.

I continued to wait for VMRC to call, but tried to have patience, knowing the LORD was working things out. I could not stick my hand in "the mix", or I'd mess things up. Believe me; I slapped my own hand a couple of times so not to pick up a phone to call them.

Ramona returned from her trip and had an "offer" drawn up for me. I accepted the job right away, very excited! "Wow, I get to work at this gorgeous place, Sunnyside" I thought as I cherished the new beginning to be. I really had no idea what was awaiting beyond those doors for me.

Back at home that very same day, I received a quite disturbing call: "Hello?" I answered, "Yes, is this LuAnn Caperton?" the harsh voice startled me at first. "Yes. This is LuAnn." I timidly responded. "Well, you need to get down here so we can get a copy of your drivers license or I.D." she fussed and grumbled on. "Why haven't you come down here? It's your responsibility to bring that thing in." she charged.

I was taken aback by this woman's accusatory claims and was also mighty confused at this point; for I had no idea what she meant. "Um . . . and where are you from?" I asked, slow and timid. "Avante", the angry woman growled. "Why haven't you come by here to fill out your paperwork?" she continued. I again, fumbled for words to say. "Well, I had no idea I was *suppose* to fill out paperwork and I've taken a position somewhere else." "Oh, well," she stopped her barking and then just stated "Okay." The woman had suddenly shut up her insults and her voice became solemn in a way. After hanging up with her, I wondered, "If she's THAT harsh on the phone; how would it have been to work for them?" I shuddered at the thought.

I did eventually receive a call from VMRC for that second interview a couple of weeks later, but let them know also, that I had taken a job elsewhere.

The time I spent at Sunnyside Presbyterian Retirement Community was rich with experiences: I started off working on the 3rd floor Skilled unit, then I began to help on other floors and in the more independent areas of the facility. Other times I worked overnight shifts in their Alzheimer's unit and once had the opportunity to do a commercial for Sunnyside on the air.

My supervisor Edie, began needing someone to fill in for her, during some "Doctor Days". I told her I'd like to learn more about what she did and the next thing I knew, she was training me for that position. While filling in for, or helping Edie out, there were two or three doctors I prepared clients for. But the two that I worked most closely with were from Rockingham Family Physicians! One was Dr. Whitman and then, yes, the other was Dr. Godshall! (from Chapter 39!)

Once I tagged along with Cori to help speak at a local Nursing School, in hopes of recruiting new graduates for staff. We also took part in a Health Care Day for a packed elementary school later that year. The stream of blessings just kept coming, and my employer paid to send me to a specific class. This class enabled me to become one of the CPR Instructors of the large SPRC staff. And although I never thought I'd be paid for any acting abilities, I was; as I played a 'Bad Nurse Character' in the skits for "orientation" days that were held every 4 weeks.

During the month of May each year, Nurses all across the country are honored for their service toward mankind. In 2008, I was able to participate in a special way during that celebration. Working alongside Ministerial Staff and the Director Of Nursing, I helped give out treats each day to Nurses during their working hours. In a grand finale, a service was held especially for these chosen staff. I was secretly allowed to create a heart felt letter, speaking for all Sunnyside Community and other employees.

The Lord led us through one door and then another as I was asked to fill in once for Chaplin Paul. My husband and I were able to begin a regular Bible Study at Sunnyside later. It was called, "I Want To Be More Like Jesus."

You must be thinking that things were always so bright and joyous at Sunnyside. But just as I mentioned a few chapters back, in this world where there's good, there's going to be some bad. And with this balance we experience, where life sometimes leaves us happy, it can also make us sad.

Ms. Koontz, one of our residents at Sunnyside, was a dear and kind lady. She had no children of her own. She had practically raised her niece, Ramona, the Director of Nurses, alone.

When she heard of a celebration scheduled for her niece, the D.O.N., Ms. Koontz didn't know just what to get for her that would express how she felt. So, one night, when Ramona had gone home, she and I secretly made a stepping stone for her. With Ms. Koontz's handprint in the middle, and special words framing the edges, the eight-sided stone was completed, hid and locked in the medication room in a cabinet to dry.

When the Day of Celebration came, Ms. Koontz enjoyed watching Ramona being honored from her reserved table up front. Afterwards, she presented her niece with the large colorfully wrapped box. Ramona's face was totally indescribable, as she unfolded the bright tissue paper covering her aunt's creation. She admired the variety of inlayed gemstones, and the impression that her aunt's palm had made, but as she read the words surrounding it all, she was moved to tears; for on the stone, it said:

I Held Your Hand, You Held My Hand

Less than two weeks after presenting her niece with this personalized and cherished gift, Ms. Koontz fell asleep one night, and went home to be with the Lord.

When asked to speak at her memorial, I was honored and blessed to know, that when I would speak of Ms. Koontz that day, I could tell everyone where she had gone. And with her Aunt's departing gift, securely in her hands, Ramona was at perfect peace with God's ultimate plan.

I couldn't help but remember Who had chosen where I would "nurse". As I looked over the people, the situations and opportunities in my mind, I could see how He'd grown the fruit.

There was several times the Lord allowed me to minister to folks during their last days. And each time they went, I was reminded of the Truth that I was only a breath away from being with them. Sitting by their side one moment, and looking upwards the next, I could almost see them bid us goodbye. Oh, how I, longed for Home.

Chapter Forty-five

Did We Do The Right Thing?

Blessed are they that mourn: for they shall be comforted. Blessed are the pure in heart: for they shall see God. Matthew 5:4 & 8

It was late summer of 2008. Kathy had moved out again. And although she was the youngest of my children, she was quite the independent one; actually the replica of her mom at that age. Joshua, the oldest, decided it was time he also sprout some personal wings. He let us know that he too, would be looking for a place of his own. Now, at age 23, it seemed I would be expecting, almost waiting for decisions such as these to be made; after all, that's what parents do; they birth, they train, and they let go. But somewhere in those years of "training", you begin to 'hang on', look at them with respect and truly enjoy who and what they have become. So, when Joshua made this announcement, it was not an easy pill for me to swallow.

We had just begun to play music together; Joshua on guitar, and I on the keyboard. My son had just begun sharing with Carlos and I, wonderful Truths from God's Word; revealed through studying, dreams and tough experiences he'd gone through. "Why now?" I quietly cried to my husband. "Why does he have to leave now?" I had been faithful to my promise to the Lord, I'd made when they were small. It seemed just when I had begun to enjoy the "fruits" of my labor, the last of my precious offspring was sprouting his wings.

So, I do what "brave parents" do everyday of the year; I gave my hurt up to the Lord and, well, I began to "look at the Bright Side". THE BRIGHT SIDE; It sounds like a hotel one checks into when the world around you turns bleak; Grey, cloudy, sometimes rainy? You know what I mean, don't you? I had reached that place.

"I should have listened to my Dad, I guess." pouting a little to Carlos. "He told me that the children would be moving out soon, and we may want to just stick with the small house on Rockingham Drive." He looked at me compassionately as I continued.

"I just wanted a larger place that everyone could have their own space and the big yard for family gatherings, so that we could all have fun together." Carlos sympathized. "I know, honey. It served its purpose for a time."

Carlos began to look at our future possibilities. "You know, these heating and A/C bills are eating up our finances. Perhaps we can look for a smaller place." He continued to try to give me a different outlook on things. "Hey, that building out there wouldn't have been turned into a witnessing billboard if we hadn't moved here" He was referring to the large building behind our house, that we'd painted a couple of years earlier. Carlos was a person of strong faith and knew just what to say to turn the tide. "Okay, you're right honey; it *is* awesome, isn't it? And getting a new place will be a fresh start for us." The thought of it motivated me, which took my mind off my "soon to be empty nest" for a while.

When we arrived at church the next Sunday morning, we made it a point to ask Shyrita if there were any empty apartments in her building. Shyrita and Charity lived only a couple of blocks *from* the church; Having a place that close, would have been very convenient for us, as our church had services quite often. "No, not to my knowledge" she smiled. "But I have the landlady's phone number if you'd like to call and ask her." Shyrita helpfully offered. "Well, alright. That sounds good. We've seen *your* apartment and something like that would be a perfect size for us." I said.

After we were dismissed from morning service, we drove the normal route, through the beautiful green blocks of Dayton, heading toward home. Looking to the right then the left at the four-way stop, our eyes fixed on the yard of the apartment building we'd inquired about only moments earlier. "Look! Look honey over there!" I exclaimed. "I see!" Carlos smiled as he took in the unexpected view. Right before our very eyes, was a large moving van parked on the lawn at the apartments! We continued on past, but I phoned Shyrita and told her what we'd seen. She tried to figure out which apartment was being vacated, but was not sure. She encouraged us to call the landlady as soon as possible to inquire, so we did it promptly; "Hello? Yes? Mrs. Lowe? My name is LuAnn Caperton and I was wondering about the van outside your apartments." "Yes?" she answered matter-of-factly. "Do you have an apartment coming opened Mrs. Lowe? Because if you do, my husband and I were just asking Shyrita, Charity's roommate . . ." "Well" she said, "The small one that's being renovated today, is already taken." "Aw." I replied, disappointed. "But I'm going to have a "two bedroom" coming open this week. What did you say your name was again?" "LuAnn Caperton" I replied. "I do have one other person that has called about it, and so she is in line before you, you must understand." "Oh, yes ma'am, I understand." I respectfully replied. "So you've seen Charity's apartment, have you?" she quizzed. "Yes ma'am and we really like it. Is the other one laid out the same way?" "Yes, it is, but just turned the opposite direction." After a pause, she asked, "Would you like to see it?" "Oh, yes! We would Mrs. Lowe; very much!" "Okay then, but the cleaning lady hasn't come yet and the painter hasn't quite finished painting." she informed us. "Oh, that's quite alright. We just want to see it." I exclaimed. So the next day, after praying for the Lord's Will, and with knots in our stomachs, we went to meet Mrs. Lowe at the reddish orange brick building on College Street. The upstairs apartment had wood floors in all rooms except the kitchen and bath. She had not said anything about pets, and I wasn't going to ask. Although Carlos only expressed his excitement through wide eyes and smile when Mrs. Lowe was not looking, she could see how obvious it was for me; I adored the place. "Mrs. Lowe, if the girl that is ahead of us changes her mind, we would like to be considered as future tenants" I was explaining. "Well, if you want the apartment, . . ." she hesitated, then continued, "it's all yours; that girl never called me back to come see it."

I wanted to jump up sky high; for Carlos and I had prayed for the Lord's will, knowing He would not allow this to come about if he didn't want us to be there. And the apartment was only a couple of blocks from church! How awesome!

As we were leaving, I thought it was just too good to be true. I told her that we could write her a check for a deposit on the apartment, so she would hold it for us. Mrs. Lowe grinned as if she knew what I was thinking and worried about. Looking straight into my eyes, the jolly middle aged woman put out her chunky hand and said, "At my church, we call each other sister and brother; and we close all our business dealings with a handshake." Surprised at her genuine Christianity and trust, Carlos shook her hand, and then I did. I was so overcome with joy at that moment, I wrapped my arms around her and said, "Thank you; thank you so much", then I wiped away the embarrassing tears from my eyes.

In December of 2006, we moved in with only KiKi, our oldest cat, but it was not long before we had a total of 4 again. And that's in another story. *Read the book: Bucky Boy

Our house on Hamlet Drive had not sold prior to our moving from it. Joshua had decided to rent the house from us for a small amount per month until he could find a place of his own. We thought it was a good 'trade-off', having someone to take care of the yard and keep an eye on the house until we found a buyer.

December, January and February had gone by and finances were a little tight. Carlos and I both were working hard to keep both rent and house payment up, but it was getting tougher with each month that came and went. In our dismay, one day, doubts that we had truly heard from the Lord finally surfaced.

"Carlos, honey, do you think we did the right thing moving here to Dayton?" Carlos looked at me with thoughtful eyes, as if pondering the question himself. "LuAnn, it's going to be fine. Just trust the Lord." "But honey, maybe I just wanted to escape the pain I felt of the children leaving home and maybe I just wanted to run away from it all . . . ." "LuAnn. No, don't do this to yourself. We made the right choice. I know it's tough, but it will get better. Just trust God."

Having been sick with bronchitis in December, and then being away from both of my children, I was mentally, physically and emotionally drained. Carlos was a "Rock" at times, when I felt like such a wimp.

Later that night, Carlos had gone into what was considered his girls' room. He was trying to find something that hadn't been unpacked yet. Samantha and Samanda stayed with us every other weekend, but there were still a few boxes in the corners of their room. As he turned on the overhead light attached to a ceiling fan, digging through boxes, he found what he had been searching for. But when he went to pull the dangling chain again, to turn the light off, he took a closer look. "Honey, come here. I want you to see something." He said. "What?" I hollered half interested from the couch in the living room. "I said I need for you to come here! You have GOT TO SEE THIS!" he responded with even more enthusiasm.

I slid down off my comfy cushion, and my bare feet made a funny rhythmic sound as I plopped them one after another across my much-loved wooden floor. "What?" I said, sarcastically tilting my chin back, with squinting eyes, keeping me from being blinded by the bright light above my head. "Here! Look here!" he eagerly announced, as he grasped the round pulley, dangling from the chain. Then I read it: **SMC** and the other side **SMC**

SMC and SMC

"Carlos! Carlos!" I laughed so hard, I cried. "We ARE supposed to be here!" Together we shouted, "It's the girls' initials! It's the girls' initials!" for their names are:

Samantha Marie Caperton & Samanda Mary Caperton

"SMC and SMC"

I never doubted the move again. It was not long after that night that the house on Hamlet Drive sold. All accounts and balances were paid off and for the first time in years, together or apart, we were _totally_ debt free.

Chapter Forty-six

Grace

I call heaven and earth to record this day against you, that I have set before you life and death, blessing and cursing: therefore choose life, that both thou and thy seed may live: Deuteronomy 30:19

It's difficult to know how this chapter should begin, for it is not an easy thing to speak of the "regrets" in one's life:

If you will thumb back over chapter 7, you will remember the 'horrors' of how low one can go to hide their sin.

I have heard, and taken notes on, many pastor's sermons. Some, I may have forgotten, while others have helped me minister to others, as I have been *ministered to* by them. One sermon, however, that I will *never* forget, and has stayed with me each day since I heard it is: *The Effects of sin.* The pastor that shared this with his congregation explained it so well: Sin is energy going in the *wrong* direction; that is, in the *opposite direction* of what energy was created to do. An example would be: Someone being given a supervisory position on their job, which should be used to assist and motivate those he has been placed over. But instead, he uses that position to become lazy and verbally abusive to those beneath him; using his authority unjustly.

Yes, sin is energy going in the wrong direction. But Jesus has paid the price for that sin. So, when we repent of our sin, the LORD is faithful to forgive us of that sin.

Some folks may be asking: Well, if He forgives me of sin when I ask, then what stops me from doing the same thing; committing the same sin everyday, knowing He is going to forgive me for it when I ask? And that is a *great* question. Here is your answer:

Each time we do commit a sin, we may ask forgiveness for it. He, as I said, is faithful to forgive you, but, the answer to your question is: His forgiveness of our sin does not take away the *consequence* of our actions *in* that sin.

To give you an example, for this one, I'll use my favorite woman Evangelist: Joyce Meyer.

Joyce Meyer is an awesome woman of God. She has taken some hard knocks in her life, and probably dished out a few of her own to others, but she uses those past experiences as stepping stones to preach and to reach souls for Christ. Joyce Meyer has shared many times how she knows she has a "Big Mouth"; she loves to talk, that is.

In her early years, she used that "energy" and that "mouth of hers" to "talk back" to people, to gossip, to complain, etc. When the LORD began dealing with her heart about how she used the energy He had given her, and the "gift" of being an "outspoken" person, in the wrong way, she realized what she had been doing, repented and now, uses that energy and "Big Mouth" of hers (as she calls it) in a positive manner; that is, to tell others *about* Christ, and how much He loves them.

But let's step back and take a look: If she gossiped about someone or told someone off, repented of what she had done, she was forgiven. But what were the repercussions of her actions? A loss of friendship, distrust of others, the list goes on. So, yes, she repented of the sins committed by her heart and mouth, but she was left with a mess. God, in His time CAN repair damage done in relationships, for example, but if we had not committed the sin to begin with, our lives and the lives of others would not have had to suffer the effects. Understand? And what if someone she spoke harshly about or to, had died in an accident that day. Would the harm be repairable then? Only God knows. Point taken. (Read book: "Me and My Big Mouth!" by Joyce Meyer)

And so it is with *us*! So many Christian authors have repeated the quote:

> *(The Lord) He loves us the way we are, but loves us too much to leave us that way.*

So, having discussed this matter, I will continue with the chapter:

In Chapter 9, I shared with you, that I thought the LORD would perhaps not allow me to have another child, because of what I did to the first one He'd given me. And if you will remember, even back then, I knew that He would have been "Just" in withholding that privilege from me; being a mother again. But He did have mercy on me, blessing me with 2 more children. (And more if you have paid attention!) You may be thinking that I "got away without punishment; without repercussions of my sin in Chapter 7, but there are things I am not at liberty to share at this time, that tell me otherwise. Perhaps in the next book, I will have permission to explain. But I do want to leave with you evidence of the Awesomeness of God's Grace; by sharing an example of what He does, when a sinner comes to repentance.

It had been back in the year 2000, when I decided I wanted to help out at a local Pregnancy Center in Harrisonburg. I'd checked with the staff in this facility, and they were happy to be able to train me. "First, LuAnn, you must go through a class that you will be teaching at times, just to experience it for yourself." I was thrilled to get started, for I wanted to somehow prevent young girls and women from making the same mistake that I had made years earlier. And although we would not be making the "decision" for the women we would be helping, I knew at least they would be armed with the facts when they made that so-called "choice" the government has given them.

So, I began to take the class that was required. My instructor, who we will call "Lisa", went over a different lesson each week that actually dealt with women's choices in God's Word. Sometimes, there were highlights on repentance, God's forgiveness and how we must forgive ourselves. After each meeting, I'd take home the booklet, and study for the next lesson. Sometime during the course of it all, I knew the LORD was speaking to *me* ! *My* plan was to help *others* make the right choice, but something was reaching down into *me* instead, and into the places of my heart that I had not dared to look upon since 1982; The LORD was touching and healing ME!

On one of the last couple of times we were scheduled to meet, I was told that we were going to have a "memorial service" for my child. Lisa told me that if there was something I wanted to say to him or her, that I should be thinking about it, and perhaps write it down.

When the evening came to have the special service, I brought in a letter along with small gifts that I would have given my baby. I also had picked out the name "Chris" for my child. You see, if it was a boy, I wanted his name to be Christopher Thomas, after my Dad and if it was a girl, I wanted to call her Christina Shan, after my mom; hence the name "Chris" fit perfectly. Placing the items I'd brought, into a small, specially prepared box, the service was started.

Lisa and I prayed at the beginning. I asked God and "Chris" for forgiveness. I was allowed to read the letter I'd written to my child, while I sat by a small lighted candle in the room. A beautiful song was playing in the background.

I thanked Lisa for this, much-needed gesture, and we hugged and parted ways.

The "study" of women's choices in God's Word had come to an end, but a miracle had happened in my life; for I had found forgiveness and healing through the LORD Jesus Christ and His ministry at Harrisonburg Pregnancy Center.

After truly facing what I had done, and knowing just how special a precious life is, I still wanted to know one thing about the child I had let go. I phoned several facilities in Greensboro, searching for the place I'd gone in 1982. My search came to halt, when I discovered that the abortion clinic had been shut down. That was definitely GOOD news, of course! One less facility means thousands of lives saved. I was glad for that. "I suppose I will need to let my question rest." I conceded. *But I continued to wonder: "What was the gender of my child?"* "It must be so selfish of me, to have wanted to pursue the answer to that question." I thought. So, I placed my desire back on the shelf and tried to be satisfied with the small reminder I'd displayed:

Children are a gift from God.

In the thin squared magnet, the center was cut out for a picture. In it, I simply wrote, **"CHRIS"**

A couple of years had passed since I'd attended the class that Lisa had held, when "out of the blue" I had a dream. In it, there was a group of small children gathered around a man in the front of a sanctuary. As I looked on, from a short distance, in the dream, one little girl turned her face toward me. I noticed her sweet smile, then her bouncy blonde hair, cute frilly dress and chunky little legs. Her gentle manner touched me, as her eyes met mine, and then I woke from my sleep. It was one of those dreams that just doesn't leave, when you get up and get ready for the day. I thought many times about why the girl seemed familiar, recalling her in detail from my dream. As I continued to work at home and on the job, just following a regular routine, suddenly, a "flash" of her came in my mind. It was her! And she looked like me! I had seen old pictures of myself when I was a child; and I now knew who that little girl was. Just like *that*, it was revealed that she was my 1st child! My desire to know if it had been a boy or girl had been answered in God's time; and now that I knew she *was* a girl, I could give her the name that I had picked out. It was Christina Shan.

Each year after that, on April 17th, I gave remembrance of my children's sister. The gestures started out small; I had given a dollar when asked to, at Food Lion to help one of the "Children's Hospitals". But with each year, they became somewhat bigger; like purchasing a "Passion of the Christ" book to place at Rockingham Memorial Library, in Harrisonburg. In 2006, Christina's grandmother, who she was named after, purchased White Bibles in her memory. They were for the nursing students that were graduating that year with me.

You may think it's all my imagination or a strange coincidence: that's all. But be patient with me and my "journalings", for there is more: read on.

In 2007, I learned that Joshua's girlfriend was going to have surgery. They suspected cancer in her Thyroid, and had removed a portion of those glands. Although I did not know Krista well, Joshua had spoken of her often. I was about halfway through nursing school at the time of her "sickness" and wanted to "be there" for them, if needed. So it was not a surprise for them that I came by the hospital to check on her; there I found Krista sleeping and Joshua was by her side.

As my son and I moved to a corner in Krista's hospital room, he told me of what he'd learned so far, about her prognosis and what more they'd planned to do. We whispered quietly to each other exchanging words with sporadic pauses. We made our way back over to where Krista was laying in bed; she was hooked up to a couple of monitors. While Joshua sat at Krista's side I stayed some distance away. Her long brown hair framed her face, and somewhat hid the bandage on her throat. The gown she wore was the typical white with little blue flowers. They moved up and down as she took each breath; she seemed to be sleeping so peacefully.

As I continued to watch her in silence from a few feet away, I noticed the banded ID the hospital staff had placed on her arm. Krista made a groggy moan as she stirred. Noticing that she was reaching for more of the sheet with her hand; I stood up and came closer to help. As I pulled the covers from around her feet to give her more at the top, I saw her last her name on the bracelet. "Armentrout" it said. After she seemed to be comfortable again, and breathing like she'd gone back to sleep, I looked over the other words on the thin plastic ID. It read:

Armentrout, Krista Shane

As my eyes shut and opened again trying to adjust, I whispered, "This can't be right", "Joshua, is that really her name?" my son seemed confused, saying, "Yes, why?" I explained to him that the sister he had, in heaven had a name very similar to hers. He'd known a little about my past, and was surprised as I explained.

Krista Shane and Christina Shan

Krista was eventually released from the hospital, but had more medical procedures to undergo. She did have cancer of her thyroid, but got better after all treatments were done.

The next year, Joshua and Krista were engaged and I was so proud of my son. Krista, you see, was a perfect match for this responsible, yet silly young man. I made sure I taught her how to "fake him out" when they were "pick fighting" like we had when he was younger.

BUT WAIT! That's *still* not the end of the story! Oh yes, . . . there's even more!

When Joshua and Krista got engaged, they were to take a year to make Wedding Plans. Krista is very artistic and creative, so she began making, right away, much of the items that a Perfect Bride would have in her wedding. There were placement cards, invitations and a bouquet completed months before the planned date arrived.

Problems seemed to come out of the woodwork though, beginning halfway through that year. Work, family matters, and a few unsettled folks seemed to be trying their best to pull Joshua and Krista apart. But the harder the struggles tugged, the more determine these two became, to remain together, no matter what.

I had not known *all* their troubles, just a tad of what they had been through. But one evening when I'd come to visit, my son shared a lot of it with me. We were standing outside the apartment, enjoying the late spring night. Krista was indoors making us dinner; she'd invited me over days before.

Joshua continued to speak with me outside, "Mom, that's just part of all that's been going on. But if I can, there's something I need to tell you."

Of course, I wanted my son to tell me what was on his mind. So Joshua and I stood outside in the cool evening air, as he told me the story of what had happened over the past few months. Then, while leaning on the wooden rails outside their apartment, these are the words he shared:

"Mom, Krista and I have been dating for a long time, and you know we planned the wedding for August. So many things have been "getting in the way" of us being together.

We both have been so stressed over planning and listening to everyone's opinions . . ." I continued to listen intently, wondering just what he was going to say next. He continued. "Well, Mom, here's the thing . . . one night I had had enough and was tired of "thinking about it all", so I came home and was just talking to Krista, in general, you know. I asked her again if she'd marry me and her answer was the same, "Yes, silly, you know I'm going to marry you." But mom, what I really meant "Will you marry me *soon*; like the next day" When Krista caught onto what I was asking, we went to the Magistrate downtown. Mom, me and Krista are husband and wife; Mom, I mean *right now*!"

I was so excited for them; that they were already husband and wife. The news of having another daughter in the family was awesome, I have to admit. Joshua was actually surprised at my reaction, and told me that her parents 'didn't know yet'. "So, tell me Joshua! I want the details. How *was* that special day for you two?"

He explained how much fun it was to "sneak off" when hardly anyone knew. And that there was another couple that was with them. They got married too! One last question that I asked was, "So how long ago was this that you and Krista married; I mean, what was the exact date?" Joshua, without knowing just what he was saying, spouted out:

"April 17th"

Chapter Forty-seven

Shut The Door Lord!

And thou, Solomon my son, know thou the God of thy father, and serve him with a perfect heart and with a willing mind: for the LORD searcheth all hearts, and understandeth all the imaginations of the thoughts: if thou seek him, he will be found of thee; but if thou forsake him, he will cast thee off for ever. I Chronicles 28:9

Dayton, Virginia had been all and more than we had ever expected. The quaint tiny town was clad with beautiful historic homes, farmhouses and green fields. As I walked to the post office each day to check our Post Office Box for mail, I enjoyed the sound of "clop, clop, clop" of horses' hooves pulling the buggies of the resident Mennonite families.

After a busy day of planting, tending or reaping their fields, many would be found shopping at the local markets or enjoying each other's company walking along the roads and sidewalks. At sunset, there was a quiet hush over the town that lasted until dawn.

Carlos and I had become quite settled in our jobs and in our church, while enjoying the perks of the town. We visited my parents as often as 'time off' and money would allow. My sister, Cathy even planned a trip to visit us during the fall of 2008.

"Wow! What have you been doing today?" Carlos asked as he returned home from work. "Oh! You mean all the boxes? I meant to have them all down in the basement before you got home." I answered, as I pushed one more close to the door. I was attempting to make a path for him to get to the livingroom. "I just felt like rearranging a bit and decluttering the place." "Well, I know your sister's coming and you want to have things neat, but you've packed a lot of boxes here!" Carlos threw his keys on the table. "Yes" I agreed, "I don't know, maybe I'm doing "spring cleaning" but in the fall, I joked. "Well, it looks good." He encouraged. "You want to go to Thomas House for dinner tonight?" "Oh yes! That sounds great!" I answered quickly. "You ready now?" "Yes! Let's go".

My sister was coming for the fall festival called "Dayton Days" where local and not so local families, churches and groups set up a stream of tiny shops all along the main streets of the town. It would be a day of sun and fun for thousands, and this event took place annually.

This visit from my sister was unusual in that, she'd only come to Virginia to visit perhaps 4 times in 13 years. My Dad and Mom, who also lived in North Carolina had come only 3. Many times, when I'd visited home in N.C., my Dad would point out a house for sale nearby. My sister would join him in the chiding, and say, "We'll go in together and buy one for you here." And although I missed my family dearly, I felt I had been learning, maturing and growing spiritually these 13 years away. Even through my divorce, when we had nothing to hold me to Virginia, we chose to stay and learn. So, when the day came that I received the phone call from Mom, I continued to choose Virginia as my residence. After all, there had been other health issues that my parent's had experienced while I was away. From my mother's knee and back surgeries, to Dad's bouts with blood clots, I'd only taken short stints of time to come to see how I could help.

Why was it so different then, when I found out about Dad's fall? He had not been injured, nor was he sick. His pride was hurt; that's about all. But something inside me would not let me rest. I dreamed and felt drawn in some way. I thought it was only my flesh, "I can beat this thing. I just need to pray."

When mentioning this 'drawing' to my husband, at dinner, he told me that he was feeling the same way. "Well, he's not helping me get passed this" I thought, "I need to stop talking about it."

Carlos didn't leave it alone, however, and came home one day after work. "Hey, I was thinking; you want me to put some applications in at other Lowe's, say . . . . in North Carolina, just as a fleece, of course?"

"Well, you can if you want to." I hesitantly answered, "But don't PUSH it too hard. Just apply and see what happens." We knew we would not be happy or useful in a place where the Lord had not approved for us to go. So, each day Carlos left for work he'd say, "I'm going to look online today and apply if there's something opened." But the moment I heard him leaving, walking down the steps in the foyer hallway, I would get down on my knees and say, "Oh Lord, Please, please shut the door on any job for Carlos, if it's not Your Will that we go." In the evening when Carlos returned home, he let me know what he had found or applied for.

Each day it was the same; He'd leave, I'd pray for the Lord to stop the process if it was not His Will. On and on it went for at least a week.

Assuring me he would only apply for 2 or 3 different openings, I felt that the LORD would still have His Way; for if he would have applied for 10, it was more like "pushing" the issue, I'd say.

After about a week of waiting, Carlos phoned me from work. "Hey honey! Guess what?" he asked spryly. "What Carlos?" as I held the phone, I closed my eyes. I wanted to deter any distraction from hearing every word. He told me "A man from Lowes in Durham called me about the position I applied for!" then he stopped. "And?", I asked, as my heart began to race. "Well, he just interviewed me. But he sounded like he was really interested in hiring me!" "Whew! Okay. That's great, honey." I replied, excited but somewhat relieved that he did not have an answer yet.

Don't get me wrong. I wanted so badly to move back to be with my family, but I wanted it to be the Lord's doings, not mine or my husband's. After getting off the phone with Carlos, my thoughts carried me to the many times in my past when I *had* been tempted to pick up and move back home. Those times, if I had, would have been for *me*, or for the *children*; selfish reasons or perhaps a 'giving up' or 'quitting' in my pursuit of spiritual growth. This time, it wasn't so much about me, but my parents. This time was different. But we had to be sure; and that's why it seemed I was praying almost opposite of my husband.

The date was finally here that my sister was to arrive in Dayton. Her couple of days with us was so much fun. We got up around 5 am on Saturday morning for "Dayton Days". Cathy helped me fulfill my church assignment early that morning by helping us set up and run our church's booth for an hour. Then, we had the rest of the day together. We shopped a little, but prior to that, we made a trip around the whole mile "set up", visiting each booth, to hand out Christian magnets and verses printed on a card to the merchants there. Of course, we shared many of those with customers also. It was a day I'll never forget. After all our work was completed, we continued to enjoy time together, walking, eating, laughing and sharing. I told her, secretly, about the interview Carlos had earlier that week. She looked at me, seemingly searching my face to see how serious I was about moving. She knew I had turned down my family's teasing offers before. I assured her that we were just going to follow the Lord's Will.

Only two days after my sister left, my husband received more calls. He was now being considered for 3 positions, and in 3 more days, we had our answer. "Hey, honey" Carlos cheerfully said, as I answered his phone call. "Hey." Was my short reply, wondering what he was going to say next. "Are you sitting down"? He asked, seemingly about to burst. "Well, um . . . now I am." I took a seat on the couch in our livingroom. "LuAnn, the Durham store made me an offer today!" my husband shouted. My heart was up in my throat as I tried to listen to the details he was spouting out over my 'cell'. We would be leaving Dayton in only 2 weeks. "I have a lot of things to take care of!" I thought. I made a special trip to N.C. to search for us an apartment. Then, all notices were given to employers, our landlady and the church. And after 13 years away from my family, we were finally on our way home.

Not everyone in Virginia took it well; this decision we'd come to about the move. But we had sought the Lord, and trusted in Him. We'd come to Him with sincere hearts.

When we arrived to our new place in Graham our family surprised us with gifts in every room! They helped us in so many ways; we felt loved. It was somewhat adventurous, being in a different place, but there was lots of work to be done. It was almost like being on a ship on the ocean. Things felt wobbly for a while, with all the changes and getting reacquainted with my family, but pretty soon, we got our "sea legs" and were feeling like it was going to be 'smooth sailing'.

Dad had injured his leg somewhere before or during our move and had to be treated for a "staff infection". I helped around my parents house whenever they needed, but after some meds had been added and subtracted from Dad's regimen, his strength, stamina and vitals plus his injured leg, returned to a more healthy state.

Five months after our move to North Carolina, Carlos received a call from his long time friend Steve. During their 'catch up on old times' conversation that day, Steve mentioned a pastor's daughter he was dating. Lora had definitely made an impression on Steve and they had talked of a future together. Meanwhile, Lora's father, which lived in the Madison area, had been looking for someone to fill in for him a few Sundays. Carlos' name had been mentioned to him, and Steve's phone call to Carlos led to communications between Carlos and Reverend Benge.

My husband and I were invited to Reverend Benge's Soul's Harbour Church for a visit on one of the following Sunday mornings. We met many nice people and had lunch with the Pastor and his wife. Shortly after that, Carlos was asked to preach there. One Sunday of filling in for Rev. Benge—turned into several Sundays. Not long after, we found out that Rev. Benge was looking for someone to take his place in the ministry there.

Dad and Mom were doing fine at home. Their health checked out well with their physicians. I had actually begun taking a class at Alamance Community College and working at Twin Lakes as a nurse. So, when the offer was made to Carlos to become the minister of Soul's Harbour Church in Mayodan near Madison, there was nothing holding him back.

It was an hour's drive to Madison from Graham so we saw no reason that we could not commute back and forth on Sundays and Wednesdays nights.

The church was small but full of many elderly folks and children. I was having the time of my life as we ministered there; Carlos would preach while I taught the children.

Some Saturdays, we would ride around the Mayodan area and place flyers on doors to invite others to visit. We held fund raisers and had outreach youth nights at least once a month. The congregation grew from 20 to 40 in less than 6 months. The privilege of ministering to others blessed me in a way I'd never experienced. It was just exactly what I felt I was created to do. The children touched my heart each time they 'understood' the Word, and gave me examples of how they'd applied it to their lives the following Sundays. The Lord used Carlos like never before, as He led him through the scripture each week, giving him food for the flock. After only a couple of months of driving back and forth, and seeing the special needs of our congregation, we thought it best to move to Madison. We found a cute house for rent on the edge of town that suited our needs perfectly.

But then, there came the day, when "trouble" reared its head. Three people from the board had come to the retired Rev. Benge and twisted messages and literature that had been shared by Carlos with folks in the church. Carlos was asked to 'come under' Rev. Benge, or else. Carlos respectfully let Rev. Benge know that he was to preach what the Lord would have him preach and not just what "man" told him to preach or what someone wanted to hear. Carlos, when given the choice of "coming under or else", took the "or else". We left the church.

That evening, emotional and distraught, we were informed by many members that they wanted nothing to do with Soul's Harbour and their underhanded ways; for where we had been voted in at 100% by the congregation back in March, there was no voting that had taken place for the "ambush" that night. So, these folks asked us if we would please stay and hold services in a different place. Carlos and I prayed about it. We set up church in someone's closed in garage off from their home. Children's Sunday School was held inside the house. Money was saved as offerings came in until we could find a bigger place to meet.

A building was located after a couple of months. Votes were casted 'for or against' leasing the building. All voting were in favor of leasing it. Work was done on it each day to "ready it" for services. Although we were able to hold our first service only 2 weeks after leasing the building, people became less and less involved and soon, Carlos and I were left holding the Bible, a paintbrush, and broom in our hands with not much support. Attendance remained steady for a while, but dropped off tremendously during the fall months, and by December, taking part in the church's scheduled Christmas Dinner was quite uncomfortable for us. There were folks arguing over whether the dinner should be rescheduled, and why certain visitors had been invited to come to the dinner. Some were showing their resentment of not getting their way, at the dinner when it did take place; some were even angry because they had not planned ahead, and felt rushed to run out and purchase a present for the person's name they'd drawn 6 weeks prior. It was a mess. Carlos and I felt a 'rebellious' spirit that had taken hold of much the congregation. After that 'get together', attendance to church hit an all time low. With a cross erected in the back of the church yard and chairs set up for those to come, only one showed up on Resurrection Sunday. Carlos was determined and not deterred. He gave it all he had. And having one was better than those times we'd had church service alone. We were worn out, discouraged and financially at rock bottom but we just kept praying and trusting the Lord.

During the month of March, my mother, who again, lived an hour away, became very ill. She had several test done and by mid April, after an emergency surgery, my Mother was diagnosed with ovarian cancer.

Chapter Forty-eight

Though Thou Slay Me, Yet Will I Trust In You

Are not two sparrows sold for a farthing? And one of them shall not fall on the ground without your Father. But the very hairs of your head are all numbered. Fear ye not therefore, ye are of more value than many sparrows. Matthew 10:29-31

During Mom's 10 day stay in the hospital, it became apparent that she was going to need a lot of care. The first few nights Dad and I split the overnight stay with her. My Dad was not in the best shape himself, but I suppose the words "cancer" and "surgery" make us all rethink our priorities. He was a real trooper as he dozed in the recliner at her bedside.

Mom slept a lot at first, but soon was aware of her surroundings. She often told us that she was somewhat surprised at the find of cancer, but she was brave and trusted the LORD.

Early during Mom's stay at Alamance Regional Medical Center, my aunt and uncle came to see her. While they were there, Mom was in her bed. After conversing a bit together, all four of us decided to join hands in prayer. While Mom was lying and we were standing, my Aunt Jean began to lead us in prayer; she was asking the Lord to take care of my Mama, when all of a sudden, my mother began to cry. She did not shed a little tear; she was crying out strong, and loud, from within her being as she prayed along with my aunt. I had been in the presence of "Prophecy coming forth" before, and with the same voice and strength on this day, came these words: ***Though thou slay me, Yet will I trust in you.*** (Job 13:15) These words had come from my mother's lips! Tears were shed as the praying ended. I felt like I had been in the presence of the Lord. "My mother doesn't know verses like that" I thought, as I gazed upon my weak and frail parent. I knew those words had not come from my mother's flesh, but deep within her heart, where the Holy Spirit dwelt. I was so encouraged to know that the LORD was with us that day, and that my Mama trusted in Him.

One Sunday, there were at least 8 people visiting in the room at one time. Oh, don't worry; they weren't all talking to Mom at once. Some were at the extra bed near the window 'catching up' while only a couple conversed with Mom. One of the folks in the room was my cousin Jody; short for JoAnne. She had been living in California for many years and had only recently come back to N.C.

My Mother, lying in a hospital bed, mind you, began to witness to Jody. My cousin had all but given up on her Salvation prior to this day, because she was under the impression that one had to 'earn' that Salvation. But when my mother began to explain what the Lord Jesus Christ had done to pay the price for our sin, Jody began to have understanding. Drained from the surgery, medications and witnessing, Mom called Carlos over to add scripture to what she had been teaching. Right there, in the double-wide room of 205, Carlos and Mom led my cousin to the Lord. Later, as the story was retold, my mother added this: If I had to go through this, just so that one person came to know Christ, it was worth it all.

Many days afterwards, back at the house, all was being prepared for Mom's homecoming. It was only a couple of days before she was to be discharged, when I was sitting in the kitchen, talking to Dad at breakfast. "Dad, I think that bird has been trying to build a nest on top of your ladder hanging under the carport." Dad looked up at me from his bowl of cereal. "Hum." He acknowledged he was listening as I added. "I've been watching, and every morning I see how they have a few pine needles and pieces of sticks up there, but when I look again later, there's only a couple of pieces, not the pile I saw before."

Dad was still eating and listening. "When I looked underneath the ladder yesterday, most of what they had placed up there had fallen. But then, again this morning, I saw more up there. It must be either a *crazy* bird or an awful *determined* one." He chuckled in agreement. "That's really not a good place for a nest" Dad finally commented. "Maybe we should knock it down." He suggested. "Oh no, Dad; we can use the other ladder if we need to, right? Besides, birds don't stay in their nests that long. We can let it stay there, right?" "Yea, if that's what you want; we'll leave it there." He gave in. "Great!" I said, as I watched him shake his head at me and smile, as if he was wondering how such little things made me happy.

We'd prepared a balloon and signs for Mom, for her little trip home. Dad got a surprise when I brought Mom to the house at 11 am, when I was supposed to come get him for lunch and our 'shift change'. He was happy to know that his 'sweetheart' was back with him.

The first night was a little tough. We didn't sleep very much, but after preparing breakfast the next morning, guess what was in my sites from my kitchen chair? Yes! It was a nest . . . and not just a partial, falling apart one, but a perfectly bowl-formed, sturdy and 'right steady' beautiful bird's nest home! "Look Daddy, Look!" I exclaimed as mom was sitting up on the edge of the couch all groggy like. "What?" he peered around the table to get a better look at one of the orange breasted birds. "See? It's a nest! They didn't give up!" As Dad chuckled at what he saw, I couldn't help but think back at the strained relationship Dad and I used to have. See, he was a very busy man. Employed in Winston-Salem, he worked hard and took on overtime just so we could have a roof over our head, shoes on our feet and good educations. Oh, and of course, food on the table. That was always important to us "Joyce's" too. Anyway, I was the tenderhearted one; always getting my feelings hurt easily; that kind of thing. I used to think that being "sensitive" was a curse. I cried at the drop of a hat. But later, in life, I discovered that it actually was a gift if I used it right. I mean, if I cried to get my way or let people's words cut me too easily, that was the wrong way, but, if I cried for others or with others; feeling their pain and in prayer, that was what it was meant for.

Getting back to Dad though; back then I let people's words hurt me. (And I still have trouble with it sometimes) Well, who doesn't want to please their parents, right? My Daddy had a lot on him back when I was young. I saw; I sensed his burdens. I wanted to see him happy, relaxed, and rested. But even as a child, I felt heavy with his 'troubled heart'.

You can probably guess what would happen when I disappointed my Dad. Yep, it was harsh on my 'touchy and teary heart'. But that's the past, and we're in the present. Now, here I am, back in his home, although temporarily, yet all those memories are still lingering in the house; some helpful; some hurtful. But the Lord was at work with those little determined birds. He was showing me that we had to 'push through'.

Now Mom was getting a little more agile over the next couple of weeks, and each day, she made a step forward in her recuperation. Each morning at breakfast time, we'd look at how the birds were coming along. One particular morning, however, weeks after mom had been home, I thought I saw the female with something in her beak; "Why, look! She's carrying a worm to the nest!" I declared, "They must have had eggs in there this whole time!" And as Dad, Mom and I squinted, we saw the small wobbly heads come up as she delivered each worm. Getting a better look with my camera, I snapped some shots for an extended view.

"Well, they're there, for sure! And here's proof!" as I shared the photo taken with my parents. In my heart, I knew this simple, yet precious scene just out the window, was a perfect gift from the Lord. He had reminded me of my wonderful parents, and how they had provided for us all those years. It seemed each day; the birds were used in another lesson, as I understood more about families, and their ways. Just as I felt I'd learned so much from them; the last baby, as I watched, flew away.

Mother's Day had come and gone, and I thanked the Lord that mine was still here. I soaked up the time and took in the view as my parents rocked on the porch in their chairs. My healing mother smiled at me, and I remembered the words she had shared:

Though Thou slay me, Yet will I trust in you. And those carried us through the difficult months to come.

Chapter Forty-nine

A Home Prepared For Such A Time As This

To every thing there is a season, and a time to every purpose under the heaven. Ecclesiastes 3:1

It had been 2 months since Mom had surgery. She was still tired from medications, healing and the start of chemo treatments. I had been staying in the spare bedroom; living with my parents since her illness began, only returning to Madison on weekends to see my husband, take care of things at the apartment and play the keyboard for church services.

Carlos would spend one night during each week with me at Dad and Mom's, and I would see him on Saturdays and Sundays. I thought it would be kind of strange, being with my parents again, sleeping in a room I'd shared with my sister growing up. But I felt unusually calm and comfortable being there. Many nights, in my old bed, I even dreamed of being a child again.

We didn't know how long Mom would need me to stay with her or if the church back in Madison would ever 'take off' again; we just took one day at a time, praying for Mom's progress and healing and for the folks we served in Madison.

One day, Mom was feeling up to sitting on the porch with Dad and me. As we rocked back and forth, enjoying the sunny, warm weather, we began talking about the houses in the neighborhood for sale. With the economy being the way it was, many people had to sell their homes, while others were tragically taken in foreclosure. There was one or two houses down the street, and a couple for sale or rent on the block behind them. Oh, and let's not forget the one that was *right beside them*!

While we discussed the houses, I happen to mention that if *I* was to move, I thought the *one next door* would be the one *I'd* choose. "Really?" Dad asked, surprised that I would even flirt with the idea.

There had been so many years I had spent in Virginia, while my family teased me about coming home. And now that I was helping out at the church and supposedly residing an hour away, it had been a pretty good set up. We had moved to where the church had been, thinking we'd commute to help Dad and Mom as needed. But now, I had little reason to have Madison as my primary residence. We could just as well commute to the church as needed, and place our priorities, at least for now, on my parents, right? So, when the conversation *came up*, I *'spoke' up*!

"What did you say?" my Dad inquired. I tried to just sound like we were playing a game, tossing ideas back and forth, concealing my strong feelings for the place next door. Later, I found out that Dad had been trying NOT to encourage me to move back to Burlington or Graham, thinking I really wanted to be in Madison, while I, on the other hand, was trying not to show how badly *I* wanted to live closer, so that I could help them whenever needed.

Just between me and you, I knew Dad was a hard worker and was a person who would not quit on something until the job was done. However, I had no idea how hard my "Daddy" *would* work to see that his daughter had what he wanted her to have, until I spoke these words: Daddy, I want *that* house.

Carlos liked the idea of us moving into their neighborhood, for he had been doing things for my parents also, here and there, as they asked. Look, he had been away from his wife for about 2 months, what did you think he was going to say? Ha! Seriously though, he loved my parents and he's always been a compassionate, loving and kind person. Why do you think I married him?

So, as we pursued the purchase of the house beside Dad and Mom's, we ran into a couple of snags; but I had not told my parents about them. Carlos was having trouble getting a loan, but in the meantime, my Dad was secretly devising a 'backup plan'.

During the month of June, Carlos told me, "Honey, I don't know if this loan is going to pan out." His head was hung low as he demonstrated how he hates to disappoint the ones he loves. "That's alright honey. Just do what you can." I replied, knowing he was too busy to give it much more effort.

See, my Dad's plan hadn't remained a secret to me for very long. Dad and Mom kept taking trips to the bank and having meetings with their financial advisors. Finally, I was 'let in on' what was going on. And when it came down to it, they ended up drawing up a loan for us. The funny thing is that Carlos knew nothing about it!

On Father's Day, June 20, 2010, with the family gathered around, I handed Carlos a Father's Day card and a small box. He opened the card and smiled, saying, "Thanks honey. I like it." But with all eyes on him as he sat on the couch in the den of my parents' home, he lifted the lid on the white box in his hands. His eyebrows rose up and he darted us a strange, "What are ya'll staring at me for" looks, as he pulled back the paper in the container. We smiled gently back, trying not to spoil the surprise.

"What is *this* for?" Carlos asked, as he held a key with a cross on it in the air. "Read the instructions!" We all shouted out at him, laughing at his naivety. Then, he began to read: "For $600 a month, plus utilities, you can have your very own HOME!?" As he finished, he looked up; his nostrils flared and eyebrows furrowed. "What does this mean?" He was trying not to 'assume' anything, or get his hopes up. "It's your very own key to the house right next door! It's yours!" we again shouted with varied and jumbled words. "What? We got the house next door?" Carlos again inquired. My sister and I looked at each other and said, "He's a little slow, isn't he?" We both laughed with delight of this awesome and wondrous occasion. What a special day it was for all of us!

Samantha and Samanda, Carlos' girls came to visit us a few times that summer. They helped us clean and paint, pack and unpack. Many folks pitched in to help; neighbors, family and friends. But behind the scenes, the Lord had worked it all out, for the house next door had not had a "For Sale" sign in the yard. When the owner, Audrey, who now lives in Wisconsin, found out her daughter had posted a "For Sale Sign", she had made her take it down only 2 weeks after it had been placed in the yard. This house, located on a corner lot of Lacy Street and Orice, had been empty for 9 months!

Chapter Fifty

Something To "Jet" Around In

For since the beginning of the world men have not heard, nor perceived by the ear, neither hath the eye seen, O God, beside thee, what he hath prepared for him that waiteth for him. Isaiah 64:4

God's Word tells us that material things do not last. And, well, that is definitely the case with my first Saturn. It was a 1998 model. Hey, don't get me wrong people; Saturns are terrific cars. And don't *even* get me jumping onto my soap box about how they stopped the production of them. "Humph!" (My arms are angrily crossed if you need a visual). Okay, back to the story.

My first Saturn, which was then Brother Crowley's first Saturn, then became Carlos' first Saturn, had over 250,000 miles on it. A few things had needed repair, here and there in the last maybe 10,000 of those miles, but we found in late 2010, that it needed about $1,000 worth of work done to it, just to get it to keep running. When weighing all factors into the equation, we decided a newer used car may be our safest bet. Since Carlos was the one driving from Burlington to Greensboro each day to work, he took our newer Saturn, the 2002 model I'd purchased just before we'd started dating. (Remember the one in Chapter 39?)

Since Carlos was driving the newer model, it kind of put me in a 'fix' when I needed to go to one of my jobs. Since I had moved back to Burlington, I had taken on medical situations such as dressing a wound, or sitting with the handicapped, while their caregiver was away. My parents would graciously offer their Rendezvous when I needed a ride. And *that Rendezvous* is a cool and roomy vehicle! But borrowing someone else's automobile, even your parents', gets old really quick; I mean, like you're imposing on someone; so I began to look for a used car myself.

Now, I would only call about the vehicles listed in the newspaper, or online in my search, and then stop if I saw one along the way while running an errand for Mom. Gas prices have been soaring!

Once, I spotted a light blue Saturn at Maxwell Volkswagen Dealership on Church Street in Burlington. I stopped, took a test drive with a fellow named Drae. Afterwards, I sat at his desk while he and his boss offered a lower price hoping I would make the purchase. Telling them I'd think about it, and let my husband know, held them off a bit. Those statements, at least kept them from pulling out the hours of persuasion tactics I was used to prior to Saturn Salesmen.

Drae and his boss had come around the $5,000 mark, in their offer, which had been my choice of limit. I didn't return for that vehicle, but Drae kept in touch. I had a variety of dealers calling me everyday, to tell me about what they had on their lots. You see, once you let them know you're looking, they work pretty hard trying to 'make that sell'.

Most of the ones in my price range were either very old or so huge; a 'fill up' would have cost more than the car payment would have been. I stopped driving onto the lot of one Dealership nearby our home, because the salesmen would run out and bombard me with questions. I just wanted to drive through and look, and not be pressured, you know? I even had a couple of salespeople to offer to bring a car *to* me to try out. Did I mention also that our economy was hurting?

Anyway, I really only test drove a couple of vehicles; both Saturns, but I just felt uneasy about 'being in a hurry'. So, I prayed, and I waited, prayed and I waited. "Lord, all I really need is something small, just a little something to Jet around town in; that's all I ask for."

Once, I called a small car lot on Church Street. I'd spotted it on the way home from picking up bread at Aldi's. After informing me how many "great" cars he had with over 100,000 miles on them, and that they would 'surely last me a long, long time', the salesman added a discouraging jab, "Aw. You'll never find anything with lower mileage than these, within that price range." That's all he had to tell me, to get me excited, because I knew my God was bigger than that.

One day, I received a phone call. This one was different than the rest. "LuAnn?" the voice asked. "Yes. This is LuAnn." "Well, hi! It's Drae again. Hey, I know I've called you a lot, but LuAnn, I think I have found the perfect car for you!" He informed me with much enthusiasm. I waited on the line. "Okay." I said, so he'd continue. "Well, it's a 2003 VW Jetta! They only want $5,000 for it. It's been well maintained; brought to our shop for all the normal upkeep . . . LuAnn, I believe this is *your* car!" "Well, Drae, it's sounds good. So, you have it there now at the VW place?" I asked. "Oh, no, I'm sorry to confuse you. A couple that I know is selling it straight out." He explained. "It's just when I heard about it, I thought about you. You see, this couple buys a car from us every few years, and it's always a Jetta! They love them!" I was a tad confused at what he was getting out of the deal. Then, he went on to say, "It's just that the dealership wouldn't give them the trade in they wanted, so they're selling their 2003 first, and then purchasing a new one. I don't get *anything* from the sell of *this* one, but what happens is; I get to sell them the *new* one when this one sells." "Oh! I see!" I was a little slow that day. "Well, Drae, how do I see or test drive this vehicle?" He sounded so excited about it, I hated to disappoint him and not see it. "Oh, I'm going to give you their number and you can call them and set something up, okay?" "Okay, Drae. Thanks. What's the number?" I asked. This persistent, 'go the extra mile' salesperson certainly had my vote. I mean, he didn't have to go to all this trouble. Well, he must have believed I was *serious* about buying, because he had phoned me at least 5 times about different ones, but always, always without pressure and he treated me the same each time he called; not seeming to hold a grudge or find me useless because I hadn't come in to the dealership when he called.

So, I phoned the Schmidts at the number he gave me. "Hello? Yes, Mr. Schmidt? My name is LuAnn, and Drae gave me your number to inquire about your VW Jetta. Is it still for sale?" "Yes LuAnn. It is!" I could tell he was smiling. "Would you like to try it out; I mean drive it?" he continued, with a somewhat strong German accent. "Well, I don't always have a way to be able to 'get out' whenever I want, so . . ." as I was explaining, Mr. Schmidt interrupted me. "Oh, yes. Drae told us of your situation. Well, we live in Mebane. My wife or I can give you instructions how to get here. You can just call us whenever you think you are able to come." I thought it kind of him to be so "understanding". "Yes. That would be great." I commented. He proceeded with directions and told me to call him the day I could find a way to their house.

I continued to stay busy at Mom's, at my own home and at a couple of jobs I was working. I had continued to ask the Lord for patience in buying a car. I knew He was going to have to just "truly make it known" which one he wanted me to have. I knew if I jumped to "make something happen" out of my flesh, (being in a rush or let my eyes fool me into purchasing something that 'looked good', but on the inside was not so good), I would regret it in the end.

Thanksgiving was right around the corner and our families were in preparation for it. Carlos went to get the girls and afterward, we both rode to take them back to Virginia. Time flew. Somewhere during the days we had them, I phoned the Schmidts and let them know how sorry I was that I had not come by yet. I asked if many folks had come to see the car and if anyone had already purchased it. They let me know that a couple of folks had driven it, but they had no 'takers' so far.

As I was telling them that I would try to get by there soon, Mr. Schmidt paused while he and his wife began talking in the background. When his voice returned to our conversation, he said, "LuAnn, what do you think about us bringing you the car to look at?" I was delighted at the thought. "Why, I suppose that would be great!" I said. "But I hate for you to have to go to so much trouble." I added. "I don't want you to have to make a special trip. How about if you happen to be coming out this way, you can call me and see if I'm at home, and of course, if you sell it before then, I will understand." I really was leaving it in God's hands, wasn't I? Scary; it almost seemed like I was running away from this vehicle! Mr. Schmidt agreed that it was a good idea. He would call one day when they were coming to Burlington.

Christmas came quickly, and with it lots of out of town guests and many celebrations to attend. I had not had much time to think about Mr. and Mrs. Schmidt, or their VW. As I was waving at each family member and friend, while they drove away, going back to their everyday routines, I caught a glimpse of the empty space under the carport, and thought of the Schmidts and their car. "Oh, they must have sold it." I thought to myself. And I hadn't even told my husband anything about it. "Well, I guess that wasn't the *one*." I said; my thoughts had slipped out of my mouth. "What did you say honey?" Carlos looked up from his wrestling show. "What did you say?" he asked. "Um . . . oh, I said that 'wrestling' really looks like *fun*! Yea . . . that wrestling really looks like fun." Wide-eyed, I fumbled. "Oh, yea. I *know* its fun!" he agreed, as he demonstrates a 'move' for me . . . "Yea; they move their arms like this and then take 'em down like that and . . ." "Okay, honey. Okay. I believe you." See, it was better this way. He didn't know about the car, therefore, he didn't have to be disappointed.

It was 10 days after Christmas. I was cleaning up at Mom's. "We're going to take the Rendezvous and have it inspected today, LuAnn." Mom informed me. "And we'll probably pick up some lunch somewhere afterwards, alright? So if you have something to do, we will be gone a while." "Okay, Mom. I'm just going to finish up my jobs here, and go home." I do a couple of things around their house each week. My dad heard us talking and said, "I'm going to look at some of those cars on the lot at 1st Nations Auto Sales, to see what they have." "Okay, Dad." I told him, although I had seen those vehicles just a week before. And just like a lot of the other places, they had either big cars which were 'gas hogs' with pretty decent prices, or small cars with high mileage and high prices to match. But my Dad was attempting to be helpful, and who knows; He may find something there for me. I knew that if my Dad approved of a car, it would probably be the one I was supposed to buy. He's always had a great sense of discernment about him; that's for sure.

When they left and I had just completed some dusting, my cell phone rang. "Hello?" I had not recognized the number on the display. "Yes LuAnn? This is Mr. Schmidt, the person with the Volkswagen; do you remember?" "Oh, yes! Mr. Schmidt! I remember. Yes!" "Well, you told us to call you when we were coming to town, and today, I am coming to town. I will bring the Volkswagen to you. You can drive the car if you like." His German accent was pronounced, but very sweet. "Um, well . . ." I looked at Mom's house, and then I thought about them being gone and continued. "Why, yes! This would be a perfect time for me to try out your car! When will you be here?" "Hum, let's see, how about 11:30. Is that okay?" he politely asked. "Oh, yes. I'll be here." I said, as we ended the conversation. "Wow! I'm really going to be able to try out this car!" I said aloud. And I began running around making myself busy until he came.

I started thinking about something, though. "What if I disappear and my family doesn't know where to find me? I don't even really know this man!" I laughed at my own paranoia, but went with what I'd always been taught: **"Better safe than sorry"** Don't laugh! Well, that's what they always said. With that sentiment, I wrote a quick note and stuck it in my Bible on the counter, stating: *"Gone with Mr. Schmidt from Mebane to test drive his car"*, then added his and his wife's phone number.

Around 11:30 am, I stepped outside Dad and Mom's house to wait, and just as I did, I saw a silver little car driving moderately, but then slowing, as he then pulled up along the curb at the house next door.

I walked across the grass to my yard and greeted him, "Mr. Schmidt?" "Oh, yes! LuAnn!" he returned it just as heartily, as he extended his right hand to meet mine. "Well, she is a pretty one." I observed. "You ready to go?" I asked the salt and pepper-haired gentleman. "Yes. I will ride over here" he pointed to the passenger's side. "Okay" I agreed, having expected that. He explained that the keys were in the ignition and as he got in beside me, he seemed relaxed and said, "You go anywhere you want to go. The tank is full and I'm in no hurry; so just take your time. Anywhere. Anywhere you want to go." his accent seemed even more appealing in person.

I was so "impressed" by the great condition and looks of the car's outer silver body and black stick and steering column, that when I turned the key to the ignition, and heard the old familiar sound of a foreign car, I thought I was having 'flashbacks' of when I first began to drive. "Wow." I thought to myself. "This is niiiiiice!" As we took off toward the highway, I knew just where I wanted to go.

"My parents are out on Webb Avenue" I shared, as Mr. Schmidt sat in the next seat. "I'd like to show them the car, if you don't mind." "Oh, yes. You can go. Yes! Go wherever you like; I told you." The smile on his face let me know he was in it for the long haul. His kindness seemed to go beyond just wanting to sell his car. I found it refreshing.

As we arrived at "1st Nations" and pulled up into the filled lot, I didn't see my parent's vehicle. I hopped out of the little VW and went into inquire, if they had left. "Yes, they've been gone about a half hour" the woman behind the counter told me. So, I jumped back in the driver's seat and let Mr. Schmidt know they weren't there. "On our way back home, I'm going to check one more place, alright?" I asked, as I turned to read the reaction from his face. "Oh, yes, LuAnn. Yes. Anywhere you want to go." I knew one of my parent's favorite places to eat was "Grill Worx", and it wasn't far from the car lot we were leaving. But to my disappointment, their Rendezvous was not in any of the parking spaces there. I'd decided to go back home. Along the way, I made a call, "Hello, Mom? Where did you all eat?" I tried to keep my demeanor cool, so she wouldn't catch on to what I was 'up to'. And just as I pulled up in front of my parent's house, she told me that they were almost home. I got out of the car, a bit nervous, trying to sum up in my mind what to say to my Dad prior to his arrival, and in a snap of two fingers, they were there, pulling up into the driveway.

I watched my Mom's face, as their vehicle swung past Mr. Schmidt's. She was smiling! I was relieved and hopeful Dad would be doing the same. "Dad, Mom, this is Mr. Schmidt" I introduced the three, after they made their way to the curb. "He has brought his and his wife's car here, and I've driven it around awhile." Dad extended his large, still strong hand, out, as thanks to the smiling, friendly man as my Mom grinned excitedly. "Come on Dad, I want you to take a ride." I pulled, and opened the passenger door in hopes he'd concede. I knew he would be honest in his summation of it all, once he'd had a sample of its handling. "Okay! Let's go!" he agreed, as he sat in Mr. Schmidt's seat. "I'll sit back here" the generous man added, as he awkwardly adjusted himself to the backseat.

We waved at Mom and pulled off in 1st, and as I changed to 2nd and 3rd, I smiled; feeling impressed with the one I'd chosen to show my father. "It's a stick. Is that what you wanted?" my Dad inquired as he rode. "Oh, sticks are fun, I had forgotten! Yes, that's what I want." As we rode on, I noticed Mr. Schmidt had his right hand hanging onto the handle above his head. "Mr. Schmidt, I'm not scaring you, am I?" I kidded, trying to lighten up my still nervousness about Dad. "Oh no, I'm okay" he answered from the backseat. "Actually, I've never ridden back here!" We laughed as he continued to cling to the hanging upper plastic, with his left hand on his seat.

"Seems like a good little car." Daddy spoke kind of low. "How much is he asking for it?" "Five", I whispered back, "Have you thought about making him an offer?" He continued letting me know he approved. "No. But I guess I can." I was still hesitantly feeling my Dad out. We discussed how much I could put down, and when we were all out of the car, my Dad told me he'd finance it, if I needed him to. I was so excited that day! I knew the LORD had heard my prayers. He'd given me everything I wanted: My Dad's approval, financing and a 'choice' vehicle.

2003 Volkswagen Jetta

Jubile = Jubilee = Strong's # 3104 & 2986 = The signal of the Silver Trumpets

You see, The LORD had sent Dad to check out what was on the lot while he was getting their vehicle inspected, and to see some examples of what was 'out there'. With mileage and prices way too high, He knew Dad would recognize a "deal" when he saw it. And when Mr. Schmitz's wife came to meet us the next day, it ended up that she knew Mom and Dad from work!

As far as my desire for a *Saturn* goes; what's a Saturn? Ha! What is so amazing is, that just the day before Mr. Schmidt's call, I had turned 50. Fifty is the year of jubilee (spelled "Jubile" in the Bible), which includes emancipation, restoration and redemption in God's Word. (Leviticus 25:9-16 & 52) And redemption, is represented by the color none other than . . . "*Silver!*" (Leviticus 27:3-7); And had I not asked the LORD for a small car just to "Jet" around in? "Yes! I did!" And He gave me a: *"Jetta"!*

God doesn't do things "halfway". He loves us, after all. He teaches us patience, pliability and courage and like any Dad, wants the best for us. Thank You Lord, for all You've done for us. You are Amazing, Awesome and All Powerful and I Trust in You!

Epilogue

My sheep hear my voice, and I know them, and they follow me. John 10:27

Dear reader: Thank you for allowing me to share these 50 chapters about my life. These experiences, along with others, have indeed made my faith and trust in the LORD much stronger.

Some who read these excerpts will indeed, see how their lives relate; Some of you may be thinking that these things could not happen everyday, to just anyone; and that these stories do not represent a "typical" life.

I want to tell you that our God is a Big God (actually the Only God) and the instances on these pages can and probably are, like yours; For God is no respecter of persons. *(James 2:1-10)* I know. I know. When I first heard that statement, I almost took offense at its words. "No Respecter Of Persons? What? God doesn't respect me or anyone?" Well, no! That's not what it means at all. It simply means He does not favor one of us over the other. And that, my friend is GREAT NEWS!

So go out, live that life that the LORD has granted you. Begin to recognize and appreciate Who He is and Where He has brought you from. C.S. Lewis recognized our life stories like this:

Miracles are a retelling in small letters of the very same story which is written across the whole world in letters too large for some of us to see.

Afterword

Cricket In The City

As we conclude our time together, I'd like to share a story with you. This story has been passed around for many years. And today, its lesson is no less true than it was in the beginning.

A Native American and his friend were in downtown New York City, walking near Times Square in Manhattan. It was during the noon lunch hour and the streets were filled with people. Cars were honking their horns, taxicabs were squealing around corners, sirens were wailing, and the sounds of the city were almost deafening.

Suddenly, the Native American said, "I hear a cricket."

His friend said, "What? You must be mistaken. You couldn't possibly hear a cricket in all of this noise!"

"No, I'm sure of it," the Native American said, "I heard a cricket."

"Whatever." said the friend.

The Native American listened carefully for a moment, and then walked across the street to a big cement planter where some shrubs were growing. He looked into the bushes, beneath the branches, and sure enough, he located a small cricket.

His friend was utterly amazed. "That's incredible," said his friend. "You must have superhuman ears!"

"No," said the Native American. "My ears are no different from yours. It all depends on what you're listening for."

"But that can't be!" said the friend. "I could never hear a cricket in this noise."

"Yes, it's true," came the reply. "It depends on what is really important to you. Here, let me show you." He reached down into his pocket, pulled out a few coins, and discreetly dropped them on the sidewalk. And then, with the noise of the crowded street still blaring in their ears, they noticed every head within twenty feet turn and look to see if the money that tinkled on the pavement was theirs.

"See what I mean?" asked the Native American. "It all depends on what's important to you."—Author Unknown

This story is a "Powerful one"! For, you see, just as the Native American man in the city was able to hear a cricket, and the people were able to hear the coins fall to the sidewalk, we, who choose to put the LORD first, can and will hear His voice above everything else.

And when you hear Him, obey His voice, for He, as our Father, desires the Best for us.

Thank Him; Love Him; Serve Him; and Bring Glory to His Holy Name.

Father's Love Letter

My Child . . .

You may not know me, but I know everything about you . . . Psalm 139:1 I know when you sit down and when you rise up . . . Psalm 139:2 I am familiar with all your ways . . . Psalm 139:3 Even the very hairs on your head are numbered . . . Matthew 10:29-31 For you were made in my image . . . Genesis 1:27 In me you live and move and have your being . . . Acts 17:28 For you are my offspring . . . Acts 17:28 I knew you even before you were conceived . . . Jeremiah 1:4-5 I chose you when I planned creation . . . Ephesians 1:11-12. You were not a mistake . . . . Psalm 139:15-16 For all your days are written in my book . . . Psalm 139:15-16 I determined the exact time of your birth and where you would live . . . Acts 17:26 You are fearfully and wonderfully made . . . Psalm 139:14. I knit you together in your mother's womb . . . Psalm 139:13 And brought you forth on the day you were born . . . Psalm 71:6 I have been misrepresented by those who don't know me . . . John 8:41-44 I am not distant and angry, but am the complete expression of love . . .

I John 4:16 And it is my desire to lavish my love on you . . . I John 3:1 Simply because you are my child and I am your Father . . . I John 3:1 I offer you more than your earthly father ever could . . . Matthew 7:11 For I am the perfect Father . . . Matthew 5:48 Every good gift that you receive comes from my hand . . . James 1:17 For I am your provider and I meet all your needs . . . Matthew 6:31-33 My plans for your future has always been filled with hope . . . Jeremiah 29:11 Because I love you with an everlasting love . . . Jeremiah 31:3 My thoughts toward you are countless as the sand on the seashore. Psalm 139:17-18 And I rejoice over you with singing . . . Zephaniah 3:17 I will never stop doing good to you . . . Jeremiah 32:40. For you are my treasured possession . . . Exodus 19:5 I desire to establish you with all my heart and all my soul . . . Jeremiah 32:41 And I want to show you great and marvelous things . . . *Jeremiah 33:3 If you seek me with all your heart . . . Psalm 37:4 For it is I who gave you those desires . . . Philippians 2:13 I am able to do more for you than you could possibly imagine . . . Ephesians 3:20 For I am your greatest encourager . . .*

2 Thessalonians 2:16-17 I am also the Father who comforts you in all your troubles . . . 2 Corinthians 1:3-4 When you are brokenhearted, I am close to you . . . Psalm 34:18 As a shepherd carries a lamb, I have carried you close to my heart . . . Isaiah 40:11 One day I will wipe away every tear from your eyes . . . Revelation 21:3-4 And I'll take away all the pain you have suffered on this earth . . . Revelation 21:4 I am your Father and I love you even as I love my son, Jesus . . . John 17:23 For in Jesus my love for you is revealed . . . John 17:26 He is the exact representation of my being . . . Hebrews 1:3 And He came to demonstrate that I am for you, not against you . . . Romans 8:31 And to tell you that your sins can be forgiven . . . 2 Corinthians 5:18-19 Jesus died so that you and I could be reconciled . . . 2 Corinthians 5:18-19 His death was the ultimate expression of my love for you . . . I John 4:10 I gave up everything I loved that I might gain your love . . . Romans 8:32 If you receive the gift of my son Jesus, you receive me . . . I John 2:23 And nothing will ever separate you from my love again . . . Romans 8:38-39

Come home and all of heaven shall rejoice ! . . . Luke 15:7-10 I have always been Father and will always be Father . . . Ephesians 3:14-15 My question is . . . Will you be my child? . . . John 1:12-13 I am waiting for you . . . Luke 15:11-32

Love, Your Dad
Almighty God

Conclusion

If you have not asked Jesus Christ to be Lord of your life, and you want to do that today, He is there with you and waiting on you to speak His Name.

The following is a prayer that you may use as an example, to ask Him to be yours today:

Sinner's Prayer

Heavenly Father, have mercy on me, a sinner. I believe in You and that your word is true. I believe that Jesus Christ is the Son of the living God and that He died on the cross so that I may now have forgiveness for my sins and eternal life. I know that without You in my heart my life is meaningless.

I believe in my heart that You, Lord God, raised Him from the dead. Please Jesus, forgive me, for every sin I have ever committed or done in my heart. Please Lord Jesus, forgive me and come into my heart as my personal Lord and Savior today. I need You to be my Father and my Friend.

I give You my life and ask You to take full control from this moment on; I pray this in the Name of Jesus Christ. Amen.

Faith, Hope and Love

As I lie in bed so tired,
There's someone still awake.
He's busy planning ahead for me,
While forgiving my earlier mistakes.

As I sleep He restores my strength,
To gladly serve Him one more day.
I awake to find He's there for me,
He's my Life, my Truth, my Way.

Surprises fill each passing hour,
As His Love with others I share.
Telling of His kindness, my joy,
Knowing He's the One Who first cared.

Closing my eyes at night, I smile at Him,
Knowing a path today was paved,
For others to find the way to Him,
Realizing I'd received more than I gave.

Just wanted to thank Him for all He's done,
Though worthy not, I'm allowed,
'Cause He reached down and saved me that special day.
Peace forever with Jesus I've found.

LJC

About The Author

LuAnn Joyce Caperton has been spreading The Good News of Christ's Love and Forgiveness continuously since 1994. Her desire is to continue to use the God given gifts of Cosmetology, Nursing and Ministry, to bring The LORD the Glory He so deserves.

LuAnn's years of Journal Entries, on the countless ways the Lord's Grace and Mercy has ministered to her in her life, gave her an abundance of material from which to extract the stories she has shared in, "Jubilee". She has been blessed with three children: Christina Shan, David Joshua and Mary Kathrine; and three stepchildren: Kayla Michelle, Samantha Marie and Samanda Mary. LuAnn presently resides in Burlington, North Carolina.

Bibliography & References

All Scripture Verses : The Holy Bible—King James Version

Brown, Reverend Tommy—Christ Gospel Church, Indianapolis, IN—Lessons & Sermons

Brown, Reverend Tasha—Christ Gospel Church, Indianapolis, IN—Bible Studies, Lessons & Sermons

Father's Love Letter—Father Heart Communications ©1999-2011 FathersLoveLetter.com

Farris, William (Buddy)—Former Virginia State Trooper—find testimony on web at faithonthemoveministries.org/orderafreecd/

Graham, Reverend Billy—quotes

Hicks, Reverend B.R.—Christ Gospel Churches, International, Jeffersonville, IN—Tapes, Books, Notes, Sermons 2001-present

Joyce, Barbara H.—Original "Jubilee" Manuscript Editor

Lewis, C.S.—quotes

Lucado, Max—Author of "He Still Moves Stones" copywrite 1993, 1999

Meyer, Joyce—Author of "Me and My Big Mouth" copywrite 1997

O'Haran, Reverend Gus—Lessons, Bible Studies & Sermons 2001-2006

Payne, Thomas—quote

Ramsey, Dave—Author of "Dave Ramsey's Financial Peace Revisited"—Published Jan. 2003

Shields, Pastor John—People's Memorial Christian Church, Burlington, NC—Many lessons on "Connect, Grow, Serve & Go"

Spurgeon, C.H.—High Doctrine, June 3, 1860

Unknown—Cricket In Manhattan Story www.ewebtribe.com/inspiration/cricket.html

Warren, Rick—Author of "The Purpose Driven Life" copywrite 2002

Willis, Pastor Kerry—Harrisonburg First Church of the Nazarene, Harrisonburg, VA—Sermons On A Personal Relationship With Jesus Christ

Recommended books:

The Holy Bible—King James Version
Precious Gem In The Tabernacle by Rev. B.R. Hicks
The Need For Spiritual Growth by Rev. B.R. Hicks
The Song Of Love by Rev. B.R. Hicks
Finding Good In All Things by Rev. B.R. Hicks
Man's Threefold Nature by Rev. B.R. Hicks
He Still Moves Stones by Max Lucado
It's Not About Me by Max Lucado
Come Thirsty by Max Lucado
Me And My Big Mouth by Joyce Meyer
The Purpose Driven Life by Rick Warren
Battlefield Of The Mind by Joyce Meyer
Redeeming Love by Fancine Rivers

WWW.*Jubilee50years.com*

CPSIA information can be obtained at www.ICGtesting.com
Printed in the USA
LVOW080131270212

270559LV00001B/64/P